Language Handbook Worksheets

Additional Practice in Grammar, Usage, and Mechanics

*Support for the Language Handbook
in the Student Edition*

Introductory Course

HOLT, RINEHART AND WINSTON

A Harcourt Education Company

Orlando • **Austin** • New York • San Diego • Toronto • London

5 6 7 8   1689   14 13 12 11 10

4500235645

TABLE OF CONTENTS

LANGUAGE HANDBOOK 1
THE PARTS OF SPEECH

LANGUAGE HANDBOOK 2
AGREEMENT

LANGUAGE HANDBOOK 3
USING VERBS

LANGUAGE HANDBOOK 4
USING PRONOUNS

LANGUAGE HANDBOOK 5
USING MODIFIERS

LANGUAGE HANDBOOK 6
THE PREPOSITIONAL PHRASE

LANGUAGE HANDBOOK 7
SENTENCES

LANGUAGE HANDBOOK 8
COMPLEMENTS

LANGUAGE HANDBOOK 9
KINDS OF SENTENCES

LANGUAGE HANDBOOK 10
WRITING EFFECTIVE SENTENCES

LANGUAGE HANDBOOK 11
CAPITAL LETTERS

LANGUAGE HANDBOOK 12
PUNCTUATION

LANGUAGE HANDBOOK 13
PUNCTUATION

LANGUAGE HANDBOOK 14
PUNCTUATION

LANGUAGE HANDBOOK 15
SPELLING

LANGUAGE HANDBOOK 16
GLOSSARY OF USAGE

TO THE TEACHER

This booklet, *Language Handbook Worksheets,* contains practice and reinforcement copying masters that cover the material presented in the Language Handbook section of the *Student Edition.* The worksheets correspond to the grammar, usage, and mechanics rules and instruction covered in the Language Handbook. Tests at the end of each section can be used either for assessment or as end-of-section reviews.

A separate **Answer Key** for the *Language Handbook Worksheets* provides answers or suggested responses to all items in this booklet.

LANGUAGE HANDBOOK	**1**	THE PARTS OF SPEECH

WORKSHEET 1 | Identifying Nouns

EXERCISE A   Underline each noun in the following sentences. A sentence may have more than one noun.

EXAMPLE **1.** The <u>apples</u> in the <u>basket</u> are for <u>Aunt Meg</u>.

1. The samurai of Japan were powerful warriors.
2. Robin received e-mail from a friend.
3. Are Mom and Dad at the game?
4. Trout and perch swam in the lake.
5. Turn off the lights.
6. Francisco has an idea for the play.
7. Rows of wheat waved in the breeze.
8. Marissa carefully cut and sanded the boards.
9. Mr. Kwan showed the class a film about Egypt.
10. The high peaks of the Rocky Mountains stopped some pioneers.

EXERCISE B   For each of the following sentences, identify the underlined nouns. On the line provided, write *common* if the underlined noun is a common noun. Write *proper* if the noun is a proper noun.

EXAMPLE   _proper_   **1.** The cabin sat on the shores of the <u>Hudson River</u>.

_____ 1. <u>Emily Rosa</u> published an article in a medical journal when she was only nine.

_____ 2. Marie Curie and her <u>husband</u>, Pierre, won a Nobel Prize in physics in 1903.

_____ 3. The iron bridge rusted after <u>years</u> of neglect.

_____ 4. Every soldier saluted the <u>general</u>.

_____ 5. The first person over the finish line was <u>Yolanda</u>.

_____ 6. Freighters carry goods through the <u>Panama Canal</u>.

_____ 7. A series of <u>canals</u> connected the fields to the river.

_____ 8. English <u>scientist</u> Jane Goodall studied chimpanzees in Tanzania, Africa.

_____ 9. Beyond the <u>desert</u> lay green valleys and silver lakes.

_____ 10. We recited the first words of the <u>Declaration of Independence</u>.

WORKSHEET 2 | Identifying Pronouns

EXERCISE   Underline the pronouns in the following sentences. A sentence may have more than one pronoun.

EXAMPLE **1.** <u>They</u> promised <u>us</u> a ride on <u>their</u> pony.

1. Do your homework before dinner.
2. Abe and she mopped the floor and waxed it.
3. The grateful king granted me a place at his feast.
4. The treehouse belongs to her, but he and I play in it.
5. We told our story, but they did not believe us.
6. The ancient Greeks often decorated their pottery with scenes from daily life.
7. The entire village greeted them after their journey.
8. The book *The Dark Child* is mine, but I lent it to her.
9. Chad took the turtle back to its pond.
10. Soon the golden trophy will be ours.
11. She looked at herself in the mirror.
12. Both of my sisters take singing lessons.
13. Bridget and I enjoyed the African dance performance.
14. These are the photos from our trip to Mexico City.
15. The coach congratulated everybody on the team.
16. You are being too hard on yourself.
17. Has somebody eaten all of the peaches?
18. Is this an Italian restaurant?
19. They think their dog eats its food too fast.
20. Did Mr. Moore give them a map of New Orleans?
21. Some of the boys amused themselves by reading their new magazines.
22. Please let me know when either of our cousins arrives.
23. Those have grown the tallest of any of the flowers in my garden.
24. Because she had many peaches, Mrs. Farley shared some with us.
25. He would not play his guitar until he had replaced all of its broken strings.

LANGUAGE HANDBOOK **1** **THE PARTS OF SPEECH**

WORKSHEET 3 **Identifying Adjectives**

EXERCISE A   Underline the adjectives in the following sentences. Do not include the articles *a, an,* and *the*. On the line provided, write the word that each adjective modifies.

> **EXAMPLE** ____*rocks*____ **1.** Colorful rocks lined the bottom of the aquarium.

_____ **1.** A fish swam through a small castle.

_____ **2.** Five catfish patrolled the bottom of the tank.

_____ **3.** A toy diver bobbed up and down.

_____ **4.** Anna gave the glass a light tap, and the fish swam toward her.

_____ **5.** The aquarium belonged to the science class.

_____ **6.** A tiny snake swam at the bottom.

_____ **7.** Naguib fed the fish a special food.

_____ **8.** Air bubbles gave the fish oxygen.

_____ **9.** The fish seemed happy in the tank.

_____ **10.** We were proud of the aquarium.

EXERCISE B   Each of the following sentences contains at least one adjective. Underline each adjective, and draw an arrow to the word it modifies. Do not include the articles *a, an,* and *the*.

> **EXAMPLE 1.** Those kittens seem healthy and active.

1. In many Japanese homes, people sleep on futons.

2. Maya picked the perfect spot for the vegetable garden.

3. The food at that Indian restaurant tasted delicious.

4. In late spring, the flowers are beautiful.

5. That story is funny and has a positive message.

6. The city of Madrid has a dry climate.

7. Please set these bowls on the round table.

8. The explorers set out into the frigid Alaskan wilderness.

9. Some peoples in the Caribbean area weave beautiful cloth.

10. Bring me the blue shirt, please.

LANGUAGE HANDBOOK **1** **THE PARTS OF SPEECH**

| WORSHEET 4 | **Using Pronouns and Adjectives**

EXERCISE A Rewrite the following sentences on the lines provided. Replace the repeated nouns with pronouns.

> **EXAMPLE 1.** Mrs. Robertson works in Mrs. Robertson's office during the week. _Mrs. Robertson works in her office during the_ _week._

1. Mr. Lee picked up Mr. Lee's Scout troop for the field trip. _____

_____

2. The best part of the movie is the movie's special effects. _____

_____

3. James Joyce wrote about James Joyce's native city of Dublin, Ireland. _____

_____

4. Cathy likes science, but Cathy prefers math. _____

_____

5. Juan's teachers recommended Juan for a scholarship. _____

_____

EXERCISE B For each of the following sentences, write an appropriate adjective in the blank.

> **EXAMPLE 1.** The puppy slept on a _____fluffy_____ pillow.

1. Mrs. Calvino offered us a bowl of _____ grapes.

2. The _____ team played until after dark.

3. The _____ farmers planted corn and potatoes in Peru.

4. _____ rings and golden coins filled the treasure chest.

5. Rich carpets and _____ curtains decorated the German castle.

6. A _____ gentleman guided us through the museum.

7. On the bedside table sat a _____ clock.

8. Only _____ minutes were left in the game.

9. A _____ smell drifted from the kitchen where Mama was cooking lentil soup.

10. We found a _____ bird's nest behind the garage.

| WORKSHEET 5 | **Identifying and Using Action Verbs** |

EXERCISE A   Underline the verbs in the following sentences. Some sentences have more than one verb.

> **EXAMPLE 1.** Our new kitten <u>sleeps</u> under the couch and <u>plays</u> in the laundry basket.

1. Sea gulls soared on the wind and dived toward the sea.

2. The equator divides the Northern and Southern Hemispheres.

3. I remember the cluttered, dusty attic at Grandpa's house.

4. The Maya of Central America and southern Mexico developed a form of hieroglyphics.

5. Call the doctor and make an appointment.

6. Good campers prepare for emergencies.

7. Dark gray clouds covered the horizon and hid the sun.

8. Antelope grazed along the grassy riverside.

9. The environmental club organized a small party in Cesar Chavez Park.

10. Joy and George Adamson worked with lions in Kenya, Africa.

EXERCISE B   On the line provided, write an action verb for each of the following sentences.

> **EXAMPLE 1.** Scientist Rosalind Franklin ____used____ X-rays in her research.

1. I _____ the money in my bank account.

2. Sunlight _____ in through the window.

3. Mom _____ my sister and me to hockey practice.

4. Our flag _____ in front of the courthouse.

5. Miss Chan and Mr. Draper _____ our float for the parade.

6. Toni Cade Bambara _____ many stories.

7. Juanita _____ the ducks some stale bread.

8. The mountain climbers stopped and _____ for the night.

9. My friend Ravi easily _____ his wheelchair around the school.

10. _____ your name at the top of the page.

WORKSHEET 6 | Identifying Action and Linking Verbs

EXERCISE A Underline the linking verbs in the following sentences. Some sentences have more than one linking verb.

EXAMPLE **1.** The large box <u>appeared</u> heavy but <u>was</u> light.

1. The colt grew fat in the lush pasture.

2. Amelia Earhart was the first woman to fly solo across the Atlantic Ocean.

3. I am very interested in the art of Pablo Picasso.

4. Those oranges tasted sour to me.

5. The sword remained sharp for many years.

6. Are Tamika and Tyrone twins or just brother and sister?

7. Learning fractions seems hard but is sometimes easy.

8. His tough words sounded brave but were foolish.

9. Be careful with my Patsy Cline CD.

10. The hamster appeared sad without its companion.

EXERCISE B Underline each verb in the following sentences. If the verb is a linking verb, write *LV* in the blank at the left. If it is an action verb, write *AV*.

EXAMPLES ___LV___ **1.** Larry <u>looked</u> sad to Jenna and me.

___AV___ **2.** We <u>looked</u> for Larry's library book.

_____ **1.** I smelled the last roses of the summer.

_____ **2.** The roses smelled fresh and sweet.

_____ **3.** Dad tasted my brother's homemade tortillas.

_____ **4.** The tortillas tasted dry to my father and me.

_____ **5.** Bharati Mukherjee is an interesting writer.

_____ **6.** She published her first book, *The Tiger's Daughter,* in 1972.

_____ **7.** Alaskan farmers grow many kinds of vegetables.

_____ **8.** Fish grow large in the cold Alaskan waters.

_____ **9.** Each student felt the surfaces of the crystals.

_____ **10.** The crystals felt hard and bumpy.

WORKSHEET 7 | Identifying Helping Verbs

EXERCISE Underline the verb phrase in each of the following sentences. Then, write each helping verb on the line provided.

EXAMPLE ___could have___ **1.** <u>Could</u> you <u>have done</u> better?

_____ **1.** Have you read anything by the writer Margaret Atwood?

_____ **2.** Does the library rent computer programs?

_____ **3.** Mr. Shapiro has been repairing the piano all morning.

_____ **4.** All students will be responsible for their own equipment.

_____ **5.** Can an artist also be a good mathematician?

_____ **6.** Nelson Mandela has become a South African hero.

_____ **7.** Fresh carrots would be nice for dinner.

_____ **8.** Will you show me the way to the office?

_____ **9.** Few people have visited the North Pole.

_____ **10.** May we be excused from class now?

_____ **11.** Do the Girl Scouts meet at your church?

_____ **12.** Yellow would have looked better on the trim.

_____ **13.** Actress and writer Denise Chávez was born in Las Cruces, New Mexico.

_____ **14.** The frogs were making a terrible racket.

_____ **15.** Should I take the towels out of the dryer now?

_____ **16.** Must I study every evening?

_____ **17.** Mr. Williams might be teaching us next year.

_____ **18.** Sally Ride had become the first American woman in space.

_____ **19.** We were just talking about the computer game.

_____ **20.** Have you seen my cat in your yard?

_____ **21.** Is your friend coming to dinner?

_____ **22.** This equation has finally made sense.

_____ **23.** The package should have arrived by now.

_____ **24.** Will you join the dance?

_____ **25.** You should apologize to your friend.

LANGUAGE HANDBOOK 1   **THE PARTS OF SPEECH**

| WORKSHEET 8 | **Identifying Adverbs** |

EXERCISE A   Underline the adverbs in each of the following sentences. Then, on the line provided, write the word or words that each adverb modifies.

EXAMPLE _____barked_____ **1.** Our dog barked <u>loudly</u> at the visitor.

_____ **1.** A guide usually helped the settlers across the mountains.

_____ **2.** Gently, the mare nudged the foal.

_____ **3.** The Babylonian king Hammurabi governed well.

_____ **4.** We read a very good Japanese folk tale called "Green Willow."

_____ **5.** The campers walked wearily through the woods.

_____ **6.** That article about Gandhi seemed quite inspirational to me.

_____ **7.** Our new bicycle helmets are unusually colorful.

_____ **8.** Keep away from the acids in the science room.

_____ **9.** Your parents will probably give you permission.

_____ **10.** We will soon be going to computer class.

EXERCISE B   Each of the following sentences contains an adverb in italics. Draw an arrow from the adverb in italics to the word or words that the adverb modifies. On the line provided, write the part of speech of the modified word. Write *V* for verb, *ADJ* for adjective, or *ADV* for adverb.

EXAMPLE _____V_____ **1.** Reid had *almost* tied the school record for points scored in a single game.

_____ **1.** The poem was *quite* beautiful.

_____ **2.** She wrote it *very* carefully.

_____ **3.** Promises should *always* be kept.

_____ **4.** The play <u>Purlie Victorious</u> was *too* funny for words.

_____ **5.** We are *so* happy for you.

_____ **6.** I have *almost* finished my report on the writer Joy Harjo.

_____ **7.** *Very* sadly, we returned home.

_____ **8.** The wind blew all the clouds *away*.

_____ **9.** Clean your room *now*!

_____ **10.** We should *not* have taken the canary outside.

LANGUAGE HANDBOOK **1** THE PARTS OF SPEECH

WORKSHEET 9 | Identifying Adverbs and Prepositions

EXERCISE A   Underline the prepositional phrases in each of the following sentences. Then, circle the preposition in each phrase.

> **EXAMPLE 1.** Lucas used warm colors (in) his landscape paintings and (in) his portraits.

1. Crowfoot, a Blackfoot chief, was known for his bravery.

2. Clayton sits in front of Marissa in math class.

3. After the play Aunt Janice drove us home.

4. Ms. Feldman went to the train station to greet her sister.

5. In spite of my shyness, I auditioned for the school musical.

6. Under the front porch he found an old hammer and a box of nails.

7. The lost hiker had walked many miles over rough trails.

8. During the long, quiet car ride, my little sister fell asleep.

9. I received a lovely necklace from Uncle Lou and Aunt Katie.

10. According to this article, Tokyo became the capital of Japan in 1868.

EXERCISE B   For each of the following sentences, on the line provided, identify the italicized word as *ADV* for adverb or *PREP* for preposition. Underline the object of each italicized preposition.

> **EXAMPLES** __PREP__ **1.** The cat had run *up* the <u>tree</u> and gotten stranded.
>
> __ADV__ **2.** Will you please clean *up* after lunch?

_____   **1.** The two friends strolled *down* the shady lane.

_____   **2.** Please sit *down* and be still.

_____   **3.** *Above* the mantel hung a large painting.

_____   **4.** A mass of dark, threatening clouds loomed *above*.

_____   **5.** Jerome waved as he rode *past*.

_____   **6.** Walk *past* the post office and then turn right.

_____   **7.** The rider slowly got *off* her horse and walked away.

_____   **8.** The man walked *off* without a backward glance.

_____   **9.** We looked *around* all day but could not find any castanets.

_____   **10.** Rosa has already jogged *around* the track four times.

LANGUAGE HANDBOOK **1** **THE PARTS OF SPEECH**

| WORKSHEET 10 | Identifying and Using Prepositions |

EXERCISE A   Underline the prepositions in the following sentences. Then, circle the object or objects of each preposition.

> **EXAMPLES 1.** Band practice will begin <u>after</u> (school).
>
> **2.** The packages arrived <u>in spite of</u> the (wind) and (rain).

1. The plane rose and flew above the mountain.

2. Gita and Mohan wrote their report on the geography of Africa.

3. Our new house is beside a big lake.

4. Did you see any rabbits along the bicycle path?

5. Do not leave the house without your boots!

6. We will learn about famous African Americans.

7. Tabia hit the ball over the back fence.

8. The carpenters built a whole wall before lunch.

9. We are planning a surprise party for her and Mr. Fuentes.

10. Meet us at the big oak tree.

EXERCISE B   On the line in each sentence, write a suitable preposition.

> **EXAMPLES 1.** You can sit _____*with*_____ Lori and him.
>
> **2.** Applause rippled _____*through*_____ the audience.

1. Coretta has received a letter _____ Aunt Grace.

2. Monrovia is the capital _____ the African country Liberia.

3. Each string _____ a sitar vibrates at its own frequency.

4. I have not seen your jacket _____ last spring.

5. A flock of flamingos flew _____ our heads.

6. *Great Expectations* was written _____ Charles Dickens.

7. Put your clothes _____ the closet.

8. Students may not talk _____ a fire drill.

9. Palani usually walks to school _____ his best friend.

10. Did you see the film _____ Brazil last night?

WORKSHEET 11 | ## Identifying and Using Conjunctions and Interjections

EXERCISE A   Underline the conjunction in each of the following sentences.

> **EXAMPLES 1.** Mr. Cruz <u>and</u> Ms. Durand work for the railroad.
>
> **2.** We stopped to rest, <u>for</u> we were out of breath.

1. Ramona or Diego will take care of the parakeet.

2. The Dutch artist Vincent van Gogh painted *Three Sunflowers in a Vase* in 1888 and *Starry Night* in 1889.

3. Do we have enough pencils, or shall I get some more?

4. Mallory followed the directions, yet the model still does not work.

5. Give these forms to Maya or Kim.

6. I baked banana bread and date bread for the picnic.

7. The Zambezi is Africa's fourth longest river, and the Nile is the longest.

8. The keyboard will not store melodies, nor will it play them back.

9. Uncle Eli threw the ball behind me, so I didn't see where it went.

10. Did Lewis and Clark find the Northwest Passage?

EXERCISE B   Write an appropriate interjection on the line at the beginning of each sentence. Use a different interjection in each sentence.

> **EXAMPLES 1.** _____*Hey*_____! Is Amy home from school yet?
>
> **2.** _____*Yes*_____, Amanda is the winner!

1. _____, the brave knight entered the forest and was never seen again.

2. _____, isn't that a cute picture?

3. _____! These finger paints are really slimy!

4. _____, is that the time?

5. _____! We're going to the beach!

6. _____, I suppose you may be right.

7. _____! Be careful of my sore arm!

8. _____! What a wonderful surprise!

9. _____, I spilled the milk.

10. _____! My great-aunt was still riding her bicycle at eighty-five!

LANGUAGE HANDBOOK **1** **THE PARTS OF SPEECH**

WORKSHEET 12 **Using Words as Different Parts of Speech**

EXERCISE   On the line provided, write the part of speech of the italicized word in each of the following sentences. Write *N* for noun, *PRON* for pronoun, *ADJ* for adjective, *V* for verb, *ADV* for adverb, *PREP* for preposition, *CONJ* for conjunction, or *INT* for interjection.

EXAMPLE _____*V*_____ **1.** Mother *plants* a garden every spring.

_____ **1.** Botanists study *plants*.

_____ **2.** We saw a *colorful* collage by Romare Bearden.

_____ **3.** Cool *colors* are relaxing to many people.

_____ **4.** Fill in and *color* your charts on the Sioux before next Monday.

_____ **5.** Did you bring the dog *in*?

_____ **6.** The storm raged, but we were warm *in* our little cabin.

_____ **7.** I am going for a *walk*.

_____ **8.** Chang, please *walk* the dog.

_____ **9.** *Slow* down, or you will fall off.

_____ **10.** This bus to Laredo certainly is *slow*.

_____ **11.** *Clean* your room, please.

_____ **12.** Is your room *clean*?

_____ **13.** Turn your papers *over*.

_____ **14.** I can't see *over* the fence.

_____ **15.** The park Fiesta Gardens is *close* to our house.

_____ **16.** *Close* the book about the Ming dynasty.

_____ **17.** Hurry! Your favorite show is *on*.

_____ **18.** *On* his dresser were two tickets to The Secret Garden.

_____ **19.** Our train to Mexico *leaves* at noon.

_____ **20.** Did you rake up all the *leaves*?

_____ **21.** I read the book Sounder, *and* then I saw the movie.

_____ **22.** *Your* lunch is ready.

_____ **23.** Roberto's favorite sport is tennis *or* hockey.

_____ **24.** Is this pen *yours*?

_____ **25.** *Oh*! You surprised me!

LANGUAGE HANDBOOK **1**	THE PARTS OF SPEECH

WORSHEET 13	Test

EXERCISE A   Underline the nouns in the following sentences. In the space above each noun, write *C* for common noun or *P* for proper noun.

EXAMPLE 1. Unlike all the other <u>states</u>, <u>Hawaii</u> does not lie on the

<u>mainland</u> of <u>North America</u>.

1. In December Derrick and his family celebrate Kwanzaa.

2. The visitor from Greece described some Greek customs.

3. Right after the accident, a skilled police officer arrived to help.

4. Her great-grandparents moved here from Puerto Rico.

5. In the newspaper, there was a story about the space shuttle.

6. Golden retrievers are a popular breed of dog.

7. "The Toaster" is an amusing poem by William Jay Smith.

8. The accident on High Street had caused huge delays.

9. Uncle Ted explained the difference between a grasshopper and a cricket.

10. Isn't Yoshiko Uchida the author of "The Bracelet"?

EXERCISE B   Underline the pronouns in the following sentences. A sentence may have more than one pronoun.

EXAMPLE 1. Jody practiced <u>her</u> speech but did not memorize <u>it</u>.

1. Tony said he liked the movie even though it was rather long.

2. I didn't see anyone I knew at the game.

3. Later we treated ourselves to fruit smoothies.

4. This is the photo album my grandmother gave me.

5. Several of the students helped themselves to some egg rolls.

6. Have you found your denim jacket yet?

7. Are those the books Ms. Sanchez recommended?

8. After Tanya arranged the flowers, she placed them on the table.

9. All of the teammates were proud of their victory.

10. Neither of them had ever tasted enchiladas before.

Continued ☞

EXERCISE C   Underline the adjectives in the following sentences. Do not include the articles *a, an,* and *the.* Then, draw an arrow to the word that each adjective modifies.

EXAMPLE   **1.** We gazed in awe at the <u>majestic</u> waterfall.

1. Tam makes warm boots out of leather and wool.

2. Have you ever eaten Vietnamese soup?

3. The afternoon at the seaside was enjoyable.

4. Michelangelo is a famous artist.

5. Russian dances will highlight the performance tonight.

6. Is he good at badminton?

7. Rosa bought a new computer.

8. She keeps the diary in a secret place.

9. The paint on the steps is still wet.

10. Do not walk on the tomato seedlings!

EXERCISE D   Underline the verb or verb phrase in each of the following sentences. Then, on the line provided, write *AV* if the verb is used as an action verb. Write *LV* if the verb is used as a linking verb. Circle each helping verb, if there is one.

EXAMPLES   ___AV___   **1.** Dad (is) looking for you.

   ___LV___   **2.** That book (could) become a bestseller.

_____ **1.** Should I bake the squash for an hour?

_____ **2.** The skunk beside the road really smelled bad.

_____ **3.** Homemade bread is delicious.

_____ **4.** Kathleen Dudzinski studied dolphins in the Bahamas.

_____ **5.** Did you hear the sirens last night?

_____ **6.** Shark fins sliced through the dark blue water.

_____ **7.** With the proper equipment, the band could be very good.

_____ **8.** Is Hadrian's Wall in Great Britain?

_____ **9.** Shall I call you for an appointment?

_____ **10.** The baby seems very restless tonight.

Continued ☞

EXERCISE E   Each of the following sentences contains an adverb in italics. Draw an arrow to the word or words that the adverb modifies. In the blank provided, write the part of speech of the word modified.

EXAMPLE _____verb_____ 1. Will he cut this expensive silk cloth *carefully*?

_____ **1.** I *foolishly* forgot my umbrella.

_____ **2.** Is this dress *too* big on me?

_____ **3.** You may play your radio *very* quietly.

_____ **4.** Oops! I *almost* dropped my glasses.

_____ **5.** The Yangtze Valley is China's *most* fertile region.

_____ **6.** Today, our history class began *much* earlier than usual.

_____ **7.** That last answer seemed *rather* long.

_____ **8.** Does the band *often* play this song?

_____ **9.** Sandy planted the vegetable garden *yesterday*.

_____ **10.** Our dog *almost* always eats all of its food.

EXERCISE F   Underline all of the prepositions, conjunctions, and interjections in the following sentences. In the space above each underlined word, write *PREP* for preposition, *CONJ* for conjunction, or *INT* for interjection.

 PREP   CONJ
EXAMPLE **1.** Nishi practiced <u>for</u> the tryouts <u>and</u> made the team.

1. Well, how did you like the roller coaster?

2. Aunt Sofia gave a talk about the life and art of Diego Rivera.

3. Many Pueblo Indians live in New Mexico and Arizona.

4. Oops! I almost stepped on the puppy's tail!

5. Would you like milk or grape juice with your sandwich?

6. Her legs were tired, yet she kept walking.

7. Julia dribbled right through the defense and made a layup.

8. Lian searched everywhere but could not find her earrings.

9. Throughout the school year, I look back through my writing journal.

10. Hooray! Michael Chang won the match!

Continued ☞

LANGUAGE HANDBOOK 1 WORKSHEET 13 *(continued)*

EXERCISE G   On the line provided, write the part of speech of the italicized word or words in each sentence. Write *N* for noun, *PRON* for pronoun, *ADJ* for adjective, *V* for verb, *ADV* for adverb, *PREP* for preposition, *CONJ* for conjunction, and *INT* for interjection.

EXAMPLES   __INT__   1. *Aha*! I found the bug in my computer program!

__PRON__   2. Is this *his* book?

_____ 1. The name of Canada's *Nunavut Territory* means "our land."

_____ 2. *They* have a book about magic tricks.

_____ 3. Mr. Williams will tell us the results *soon*.

_____ 4. Malaysia's *chief* crop is palm oil.

_____ 5. Your order will arrive in two *or* three weeks.

_____ 6. *After* dinner, we can play checkers.

_____ 7. *Return* your bus passes to Mrs. Mizumura.

_____ 8. *Ouch!* Those cactus thorns really hurt!

_____ 9. The Columbia River flows into the *sea*.

_____ 10. A *narrow* ledge circled the building.

_____ 11. The new student council representative will be *he*.

_____ 12. I have *never* watched that show.

_____ 13. Tenzing Norgay *and* Sir Edmund Hillary climbed Mount Everest in 1953.

_____ 14. Don set the table *for* dinner.

_____ 15. Puppets danced *merrily* to the flute music.

_____ 16. *Did* you *close* the refrigerator door?

_____ 17. The road *narrowed* at the entrance to the woods.

_____ 18. You didn't sound *nervous* to me.

_____ 19. *Meatballs* are on the menu today.

_____ 20. People in India celebrate Divali, an *annual* festival.

_____ 21. *Goodness*, there was a large crowd at the soccer game.

_____ 22. Our neighbors began *their* vacation this morning.

_____ 23. The pilot landed the plane *safely*.

_____ 24. How many glasses and plates do you need *for* the guests?

_____ 25. We wore our hats and jackets, *for* a cold wind was blowing.

LANGUAGE HANDBOOK **2** AGREEMENT

WORSHEET 1 Distinguishing Between Singular and Plural

EXERCISE A   Some of the following nouns and pronouns are singular, and some are plural. Identify each singular word by writing *S* and each plural word by writing *P* on the line provided.

EXAMPLES   ___S___ **1.** genius

___P___ **2.** mice

_____	**1.** animal	_____	**6.** cords
_____	**2.** igloos	_____	**7.** he
_____	**3.** mineral	_____	**8.** calves
_____	**4.** blueberries	_____	**9.** they
_____	**5.** kitchen	_____	**10.** bottle

EXERCISE B   On the line provided, write *S* if the subject and verb are singular. Write *P* if the subject and verb are plural.

EXAMPLES   ___S___ **1.** cloth tears

___P___ **2.** fish swim

_____	**1.** Felicia runs	_____	**6.** we sing
_____	**2.** happiness is	_____	**7.** fire burns
_____	**3.** people listen	_____	**8.** ambassadors meet
_____	**4.** rain falls	_____	**9.** water boils
_____	**5.** puppies play	_____	**10.** vines grow

EXERCISE C   In each of the following sentences, underline the italicized verb in parentheses that agrees with the subject.

EXAMPLE   **1.** Adventurers (<u>*explore*</u>, *explores*) the mysteries of our world.

1. Mechanics (*repair, repairs*) motors and engines.

2. Rivers (*run, runs*) down from the mountains and into the ocean.

3. We (*play, plays*) in the park on Martin Luther King, Jr., Boulevard.

4. Aunt Meena (*come, comes*) over once a week.

5. That dog frequently (*follow, follows*) me home for some reason.

LANGUAGE HANDBOOK **2** **AGREEMENT**

WORSHEET 2 | Using Subjects and Verbs with Prepositional Phrases

---

EXERCISE A   In each of the following sentences, cross out any phrase or phrases that come between the subject and the verb. Then, underline the subject once and the verb twice.

EXAMPLE   **1.** His <u>brothers</u> ~~at college in Montana~~ <u><u>study</u></u> those books.

1. Members of the hockey team are responsible for their own equipment.

2. Suddenly, a team of horses was galloping by us.

3. Nights in Alaska last a long time during the winter.

4. The translucent paper partitions in traditional Japanese homes are called shoji.

5. A crowd around the door was demanding an explanation.

6. Frequently, rabbits from the park across the street run into our yard.

7. A small herd of cattle was grazing on the plain.

8. Time limits for the test are on the board.

9. Unfortunately, a truckload of very ripe tomatoes had spilled on the road.

10. The people of the Netherlands are known as the Dutch.

EXERCISE B   In each of the following sentences, underline the subject. Then, underline the correct verb in parentheses.

EXAMPLE   **1.** Only one <u>actor</u> in all their performances (<u>*was*</u>, *were*) late for curtain call.

1. The descendants of Dutch settlers in South Africa (*is, are*) called Afrikaners.

2. All my brothers except David (*work, works*) in our parents' store.

3. China's Three Gorges Dam on the Yangtze River (*are, is*) an ambitious project.

4. Daydreams about the weekend (*race, races*) through my mind.

5. The book about the wars of the twentieth century (*are, is*) on the north wall of the library.

6. The weather in tropical regions (*are, is*) almost always predictable.

7. The restaurants at the beach (*has, have*) tables outside.

8. The rain in many countries (*fall, falls*) only at one time of year.

9. Few sculptures by this artist (*remain, remains*) in his country.

10. The hamsters in that cage (*seem, seems*) very lively.

LANGUAGE
HANDBOOK **2** AGREEMENT

WORKSHEET 3 | **Ensuring Agreement with Indefinite Pronouns**

EXERCISE   Underline the correct verb form in parentheses in each of the following sentences.

> **EXAMPLES** 1. Most of the shirts (*was, were*) on sale.
>
> 2. (*Do, Does*) any of the pens on the desk still work?

1. Each of the players (*gets, get*) a pair of shinguards.

2. Several of the picture frames (*has, have*) broken glass.

3. Everyone (*thinks, think*) the town council made the right decision.

4. In the afternoon most of the children (*takes, take*) naps.

5. All of the salad (*has, have*) already been eaten.

6. Neither of my sisters (*plays, play*) a musical instrument.

7. Fortunately, none of the equipment (*has, have*) been damaged.

8. During Hanukkah, a few of our relatives usually (*visits, visit*).

9. Someone (*misses, miss*) the bus almost every day.

10. Most of my friends (*enjoys, enjoy*) the music of Tracy Chapman.

11. Almost all of that paint (*was, were*) used for the bathroom.

12. On Mondays and Thursdays many of them (*stays, stay*) for soccer practice.

13. One of the hula dancers (*is, are*) wearing a lei, or wreath of flowers.

14. Anyone from Mrs. Shearer's art class (*is, are*) eligible for the contest.

15. In Mr. Gee's class everybody (*works, work*) hard on group projects.

16. Both of my brothers (*is, are*) watching a documentary on the Cree.

17. No one (*knows, know*) when the next test will be.

18. By morning most of the forest (*was, were*) in flames.

19. None of those cookbooks (*includes, include*) any Vietnamese recipes.

20. This year many of his classes (*is, are*) more challenging.

21. A few of the sculptures at the exhibit (*is, are*) from Nigeria.

22. Nobody (*makes, make*) better nachos than my dad.

23. During the summer, none of that grass (*gets, get*) enough water.

24. Of all my classmates, only a few (*rides, ride*) their bicycles to school.

25. Everybody on the basketball team (*admires, admire*) Coach Martinez.

LANGUAGE HANDBOOK **2** AGREEMENT

| WORSHEET 4 | **Identifying Compound Subjects as Singular or Plural** |

EXERCISE A   In each of the following sentences, underline the italicized verb in parentheses that agrees with the compound subject.

> **EXAMPLE 1.** A sandwich and a note from Mom (*was*, *were*) on the table.

1. Corn, beans, and rice (*is*, *are*) staple food items in many cultures.

2. The chess club or the band members (*run*, *runs*) the dunking booth at the school carnival.

3. Rae and they (*was*, *were*) elected to the committee.

4. Glue or tape (*is*, *are*) acceptable on these packages.

5. My friends and I (*like*, *likes*) the new classroom.

6. Only towels and soap (*belong*, *belongs*) in the linen closet.

7. Dust or water (*has*, *have*) ruined these disks.

8. Neither Hans nor his sisters (*was*, *were*) playing that day.

9. My book report and our compositions on astronomy (*are*, *is*) due this week.

10. Either moles or a rabbit (*make*, *makes*) these holes in the yard.

EXERCISE B   In each of the following sentences, underline the verb in parentheses that agrees with the compound subject.

> **EXAMPLE 1.** Neither the shirts on the table nor the blue sweater (*fit*, *fits*) me anymore.

1. Your paints and brushes (*is*, *are*) still on the kitchen table.

2. Neither the lights in the kitchen nor the microwave (*work*, *works*).

3. Both tennis and golf (*require*, *requires*) a great deal of concentration.

4. The time and place for the car wash (*has*, *have*) not been announced yet.

5. Rice and wheat (*is*, *are*) grown around the world.

6. In those days, a horse or a mule (*was*, *were*) the fastest method of transportation.

7. Both hydrogen and oxygen (*is*, *are*) elements in ice, snow, and water.

8. The lines and points on the graph (*mean*, *means*) an increase in production.

9. Either Maria or Sangeeta (*print*, *prints*) the posters for our play every year.

10. Either the kilt or the beret (*belong*, *belongs*) to Dave.

LANGUAGE HANDBOOK **2** **AGREEMENT**

WORKSHEET 5 | **Using the Subject After the Verb**

EXERCISE A   Underline the subject in each of the following sentences. Then, underline the correct verb in parentheses.

> EXAMPLES 1. (_Are_, _Is_) the <u>blades</u> on the lawn mower sharp enough?
>
> 2. There (_are_, _is_) a colorful <u>parrot</u> in that picture.

1. Luckily, there (_are_, _is_) more glasses in the cabinet.

2. Here (_are_, _is_) my suggestion for our project on the Brazilian rain forest.

3. There (_was_, _were_) two baby robins and some eggs in a nest.

4. (_Do_, _Does_) these jalapeño peppers taste good in chili?

5. Beneath the bridge (_was_, _were_) a family of sea gulls.

6. Here (_are_, _is_) the key to the mailbox.

7. (_Was_, _Were_) she planning on a raise in her allowance?

8. (_Are_, _Is_) that boy in the yard a friend of yours?

9. (_Has_, _Have_) the slides on the Caribbean islands been shown yet?

10. (_Do_, _Does_) these potatoes cook for one hour or for thirty minutes?

EXERCISE B   Underline the subject in each of the following sentences. Then, underline the correct verb in parentheses.

> EXAMPLE 1. (_Is_, _Are_) the <u>camels</u> in the animal park from Asia or Africa?

1. Here (_is_, _are_) the names of the Russian ballet dancers.

2. There (_is_, _are_) some jobs for you this weekend.

3. (_Has_, _Have_) your parents given their permission?

4. (_Is_, _Are_) the pita bread in the refrigerator still fresh?

5. Here (_is_, _are_) the rules for the game.

6. There (_was_, _were_) a big white bug under the rock.

7. (_Do_, _Does_) those old cars still race at the track?

8. (_Do_, _Does_) Jobelle know that there is only one piece of banana bread left?

9. (_Was_, _Were_) they studying about the El Niño weather patterns that have affected the West Coast?

10. (_Has_, _Have_) Marvel thought of a good name for her cat yet?

LANGUAGE
HANDBOOK **2** AGREEMENT

| WORKSHEET 6 | The Contractions *Don't* and *Doesn't* |

EXERCISE A   Underline the subject in each of the following sentences. Then, underline the contraction in parentheses that agrees with the subject.

EXAMPLE   **1.** (<u>Don't</u>, Doesn't) the <u>girls</u> at your school have a team?

1. (*Don't, Doesn't*) the word *Chinese* come from the name of the Qin dynasty?

2. Shirts like this one (*don't, doesn't*) last long.

3. It really (*don't, doesn't*) need any salt.

4. (*Don't, Doesn't*) they know about the rules?

5. A good friend (*don't, doesn't*) spread gossip.

6. Dark clouds (*don't, doesn't*) necessarily mean rain.

7. I (*don't, doesn't*) fully agree with your statement.

8. My mom (*don't, doesn't*) wear blue jeans.

9. (*Don't, Doesn't*) all ripe apples turn red?

10. (*Don't, Doesn't*) you know that the Yanomami are a people who live in the Brazilian rain forest?

EXERCISE B   Underline the subject in each of the following sentences. Then, complete each sentence correctly by writing *don't* or *doesn't* on the line provided.

EXAMPLES   **1.** ___*Don't*___ those <u>books</u> have any good games in them?

2. Sometimes the <u>snow</u> _*doesn't*_ melt completely until March.

1. The Galápagos Islands _____ belong to Chile; they belong to Ecuador.

2. Oregano _____ taste very good in a fruit salad.

3. This pen _____ have any ink in it.

4. You usually _____ touch the ball with your hands in soccer.

5. _____ the goalie touch the ball with his or her hands?

6. The movie about French explorer Jacques Cartier _____ come on until eight o'clock.

7. These instructions _____ make any sense to me.

8. Many constellations _____ appear during this time of year.

9. A polite person _____ speak in such a manner.

10. _____ he know that the magnetic compass is one of many Chinese inventions?

WORKSHEET 7 | **Test**

EXERCISE A In each of the following sentences, underline the word or expression in parentheses that agrees with the subject.

> **EXAMPLE** 1. (*Here's*, *Here are*) the instruction book for how to program the remote control.

1. (*Don't, Doesn't*) a person have a right to his or her own opinion?

2. (*Is, Are*) either Yolanda or Tyrone home yet?

3. (*Here are, Here's*) the tamales Tía Rosa saved for you.

4. Those girls on the tennis court (*has, have*) invited us over.

5. (*Were, Was*) Jorge and Ruth ever in one of your plays?

6. The batteries in the radio (*doesn't, don't*) work in the calculator.

7. Heavy rain and thick fog (*make, makes*) a boat ride dangerous today.

8. Alicia and Michelle (*work, works*) every day after school.

9. (*There's, There are*) Nabil and his friend Amir.

10. Those CDs on the shelf (*are, is*) my father's.

11. (*Has, Have*) she and Jan found the king to the chess set yet?

12. The Baxters (*was, were*) living in New York at the time.

13. Those leaves on that bayonet plant (*hurts, hurt*) my hand when I touch them.

14. (*Does, Do*) they know that the Moors are a Muslim people from northwestern Africa?

15. (*Was, Were*) the newspapers still in the living room?

16. (*Is, Are*) your mother or your father home?

17. That bell (*doesn't, don't*) work.

18. The people in the stands (*are, is*) expecting a good game tonight.

19. Monique (*doesn't, don't*) speak French, but her German is pretty good.

20. The dishes in that box (*go, goes*) on the top shelf.

21. Both of the movies (*is, are*) fun to watch.

22. All of the *Star Wars* films (*is, are*) thrilling.

23. Many people (*enjoy, enjoys*) a cool glass of water on a hot day.

24. Some of the birdseed (*has been, have been*) spilled on the lawn.

25. Some of the birds (*is, are*) eating the seed off the ground.

Continued ☞

LANGUAGE HANDBOOK 2 WORKSHEET 7 (continued)

EXERCISE B Underline the correct verb form in parentheses in each of the following sentences.

        EXAMPLE 1. None of my sister's friends (*plays, play*) volleyball.

1. Each of the chefs (*makes, make*) her own special kind of gumbo.
2. Most of the cartoons in this magazine (*is, are*) by Fernando Krahn.
3. According to Coach Lee, several of the basketballs (*needs, need*) more air.
4. Both of the Selena CDs (*belongs, belong*) to Samantha.
5. After track practice, some of us (*walks, walk*) home together.
6. Of the two choices offered, neither (*is, are*) a good one.
7. Few of the children (*wants, want*) playtime to end.
8. Luckily, none of the wonton soup (*was, were*) spilled.
9. Everybody (*goes, go*) to the park on the weekend.
10. At the end of the day, someone in the class (*sweeps, sweep*) the floor.

EXERCISE C Find the subject of each sentence, and write it on the line provided. Then, choose the correct verb in parentheses and write it after the subject.

    EXAMPLES 1. A storm in the mountains (*has, have*) caused flooding in the valley.

        storm, has _____

    2. (*Are, Is*) Danny and you second cousins?

        Danny, you; Are _____

1. Here (*are, is*) name tags for our visitors from Honduras.

_____

2. My sister or my parents (*are, is*) coming with us.

_____

3. The bell at the front gates (*was, were*) made of brass.

_____

4. Behind the door (*was, were*) a gold throne and a chest of jewels.

_____

5. (*Are, is*) the people who bathe in India's Ganges River Hindu pilgrims?

_____

LANGUAGE HANDBOOK 3 USING VERBS

WORKSHEET 1 **Identifying the Principal Parts of Verbs**

EXERCISE The following list gives the base form of twenty-five regular verbs. Write the other principal parts on the lines provided.

BASE FORM	PRESENT PARTICIPLE	PAST	PAST PARTICIPLE
EXAMPLE 1. join	(is) joining	joined	(have) joined
1. talk	(is)		(have)
2. shop	(is)		(have)
3. rain	(is)		(have)
4. like	(is)		(have)
5. study	(is)		(have)
6. wrap	(is)		(have)
7. finish	(is)		(have)
8. care	(is)		(have)
9. phone	(is)		(have)
10. grab	(is)		(have)
11. recognize	(is)		(have)
12. irritate	(is)		(have)
13. embarrass	(is)		(have)
14. spell	(is)		(have)
15. crawl	(is)		(have)
16. nudge	(is)		(have)
17. answer	(is)		(have)
18. divide	(is)		(have)
19. veto	(is)		(have)
20. endanger	(is)		(have)
21. combine	(is)		(have)
22. mix	(is)		(have)
23. ask	(is)		(have)
24. foster	(is)		(have)
25. worry	(is)		(have)

LANGUAGE HANDBOOK **3** **USING VERBS**

| WORKSHEET 2 | **Using Irregular Verbs**

EXERCISE A Underline the helping verb in each of the following sentences. Then, underline the correct verb in parentheses.

> EXAMPLES 1. We <u>have</u> (*went*, <u>*gone*</u>) to the beach every summer.
>
> 2. Two of the finalists <u>have</u> (*gave*, <u>*given*</u>) the judges excellent answers.

1. I have never (*ate, eaten*) moose steaks.
2. That tree has (*fell, fallen*) over.
3. Have you (*began, begun*) your environmental science project yet?
4. Who has (*drank, drunk*) this whole carton of milk?
5. The stereo has (*blew, blown*) another fuse.
6. My sister has (*drove, driven*) our llamas to the upper pasture.
7. Have you (*gave, given*) them your full name and address?
8. You have (*did, done*) a good job on your report about ancient Greeks.
9. The water in the plastic swimming pool has (*froze, frozen*).
10. The girls have (*chose, chosen*) their partners for the wilderness hike.

EXERCISE B On the line provided, write the correct past tense or past participle form of the verb given before each sentence.

> EXAMPLE 1. *throw* I _____*threw*_____ the ball to second base.

1. *wear* Eduardo _____ his favorite jacket to the dance.
2. *take* I'm sorry, but I _____ the last apple.
3. *swim* I had never _____ across the lake before.
4. *speak* Who _____ at the *Star Trek* convention?
5. *break* Have you _____ that model car already?
6. *come* Have the tourists from New Zealand _____ by here?
7. *write* Has she _____ her paper yet?
8. *burst* Ice _____ the pipes in the basement.
9. *ride* Before today, I had never _____ a mountain bicycle.
10. *bring* Who _____ the knives and forks?

LANGUAGE HANDBOOK 3 USING VERBS

| WORKSHEET 3 | More Practice with Irregular Verbs

EXERCISE A   Underline the correct verb in parentheses in each of the following sentences.

> **EXAMPLE 1.** The dog had (*ran, run*) all the way home.

1. The Chinese poet Tu Fu (*wrote, written*) about the beauty of nature.

2. Haven't you ever (*rode, ridden*) on the subway?

3. That mean old donkey has (*threw, thrown*) me again.

4. Carlos has (*stole, stolen*) the most bases so far this season.

5. I (*saw, seen*) some real dinosaur bones at the museum.

6. Every year we have (*rang, rung*) in New Year's Day with a party.

7. She always (*took, taken*) the same way to the store.

8. The raft (*sank, sunk*) under the weight of too many people.

9. Many tourists have (*swam, swum*) in the Dead Sea.

10. We (*wore, worn*) out the batteries in no time at all.

EXERCISE B   On the line provided, write the correct past tense or past participle form of the verb given before each sentence.

> **EXAMPLE 1.** *choose* Haven't you ever _____*chosen*_____ the wrong sweater by mistake?

1. *break*   Last night, I _____ my own record for the fifty-yard dash.

2. *know*   No one but Keiko _____ the English translation for *satori*.

3. *ride*   My sister hasn't _____ her old bicycle in months.

4. *come*   I _____ to the mall to buy a shirt.

5. *do*   She _____ her homework.

6. *speak*   Everyone in school has _____ to the exchange student from Africa.

7. *shrink*   My sweater has _____ in the wash.

8. *sing*   During the bus ride to camp last summer, we _____ at the top of our voices.

9. *fall*   Haven't you ever _____ out of bed?

10. *drink*   How many people have _____ the punch at the party?

LANGUAGE
HANDBOOK **3** **USING VERBS**

| WORKSHEET 4 | Using *Sit* and *Set* Correctly

EXERCISE A   Underline the correct verb in parentheses in each of the following sentences.

> EXAMPLES 1. The keys are (<u>sitting</u>, setting) on the kitchen counter.
>
> 2. We (<u>set</u>, sit) the chess pieces in place.

1. Did you really (*sit, set*) in the Roman Colosseum during your visit to Rome?
2. (*Set, Sit*) down and rest for a while.
3. Was your brother (*sitting, setting*) the table?
4. Sharifa (*sit, set*) the record for the mile race.
5. That book has (*set, sat*) there for a week.
6. The dogs were (*setting, sitting*) patiently at the door.
7. Volunteers had (*sat, set*) vases of flowers along the walk.
8. They (*set, sit*) the trophy on the shelf.
9. (*Sit, Set*) those books down, and enjoy this delicious peach smoothie.
10. After the game, Javier (*set, sat*) out some sandwiches and juice.

EXERCISE B   On the line provided, write the proper form of the verb *sit* or *set*.

> EXAMPLES 1. Have you been _____*sitting*_____ in my chair?
>
> 2. Frank _____*set*_____ four boxes on the porch.

1. Did the mechanics _____ these tools here?
2. Rachel is _____ in my place.
3. _____ here, and I'll get the nurse.
4. My brother has _____ a goal of memorizing ten Spanish words a day.
5. _____ those boxes of strawberries in the refrigerator.
6. Please _____ up those folding chairs.
7. Kwanita always _____ a good example for her sisters and brothers.
8. Has your bike been _____ outside all night?
9. Our cat _____ on top of my bureau.
10. I have _____ here listening to my CD of Caribbean music since noon.

LANGUAGE
HANDBOOK **3** **USING VERBS**

| **WORKSHEET 5** | Using *Rise* and *Raise* Correctly |

EXERCISE A   Underline the correct verb in parentheses in each of the following sentences.

> **EXAMPLES** 1. Tempers often (*raise*, <u>*rise*</u>) with the temperature.
>
>   2. We could not (*rise*, <u>*raise*</u>) the car without a jack.

1. Many questions were (*rose*, *raised*) about ballet dancer Arthur Bell.

2. An elevator platform will (*raise*, *rise*) the equipment to the top floor.

3. (*Rise*, *Raise*) and shine, sleepyhead!

4. Our school is (*raising*, *rising*) funds for a pool.

5. The deer population has (*risen*, *raised*) over the last five years.

6. The Japanese (*raise*, *rise*) a type of barley called *hato mugi*.

7. The victories in the first games have (*raised*, *risen*) our hopes.

8. The sun (*raised*, *rose*), and we returned to camp.

9. Hot-air balloons will (*rise*, *raise*) too quickly without ballast.

10. In our class, reading scores are (*rising*, *raising*).

EXERCISE B   On the line provided, write the proper form of the verb *rise* or *raise*.

> **EXAMPLE** 1. _____*Raise*_____ your hand, and I will call on you.

1. Slowly, the mists _____ and evaporated.

2. Someone had _____ the bridge for the tall ship.

3. The muffins will _____ in a hot oven.

4. Sugar cane is _____ in both Hawaii and Australia.

5. A stiff wind was _____, and our boat was blown off course.

6. The explorers are _____ more treasure from the old Spanish ship.

7. Samantha will _____ the shades after the film.

8. The number of films produced in India has _____ by as many as eight hundred each year.

9. The king himself _____ the gate for the knights.

10. Temperatures will _____ above 100 degrees.

WORKSHEET 6 | Using *Lie* and *Lay* Correctly

EXERCISE A Underline the correct verb in parentheses in each of the following sentences.

> **EXAMPLES** 1. The answer (<u>*lies*</u>, *lays*) under the pyramids.
>
> 2. Our dog Blackie (*lies*, <u>*lays*</u>) his bones under the sofa.

1. Three nice fish were (*lying*, *laying*) in the bottom of the boat.

2. (*Lay*, *Lie*) down and listen to this recording of calypso music from Trinidad.

3. The night before, I had (*lain*, *laid*) in my bed and dreamed of the lake.

4. Just (*lie*, *lay*) those ears of corn by the sink.

5. Pieces of glass were (*laying*, *lying*) all over the living room.

6. (*Lie*, *Lay*) some apples aside for Grandma Li.

7. Mom gently (*laid*, *lay*) the old map of Costa Rica on the table.

8. Don't (*lie*, *lay*) your books on the kitchen counter.

9. Are your clothes (*lying*, *laying*) on the floor again?

10. The masons have (*lain*, *laid*) the bricks for the patio.

EXERCISE B On the line provided, write the proper form of the verb *lie* or *lay*.

> **EXAMPLE** 1. Have you _____*laid*_____ out a route for our trip yet?

1. The Fabergé egg the collector brought from Russia is _____ in its case.

2. Last fall, the people of the village _____ seeds aside for next season's planting.

3. During the hottest part of the day, the lions _____ in the shade and slept.

4. The kitten has _____ down between the dog's paws.

5. Luckily, we had _____ a few dollars aside.

6. Before my mother came home from shopping, I _____ the rugs over the clothesline and beat them with a broom.

7. A chest of gold was _____ beneath the reef.

8. _____ each shoe next to its mate.

9. The dog is _____ in the sun again.

10. I _____ down the letter from my pen pal Yosuf and answered the phone.

LANGUAGE
HANDBOOK **3** USING VERBS

WORKSHEET 7 | **Using Different Verb Tenses**

EXERCISE On the line provided, write the tense of the italicized verb in each of the following sentences.

EXAMPLE _present perfect_ **1.** Hector *has learned* how to use the software program.

_____ **1.** The plane *landed* ten minutes late.

_____ **2.** Some African sculpture *plays* important social roles.

_____ **3.** Harry *has written* a paper about the Zuni.

_____ **4.** Koko the guide dog *had saved* her owner's life.

_____ **5.** The concert *will begin* at 7:30 this evening.

_____ **6.** Our family *has visited* the Seattle Asian Art Museum.

_____ **7.** By the end of class, Tomás *had finished* his rough draft.

_____ **8.** We *will have mailed* all the invitations by Monday.

_____ **9.** The government *established* Yellowstone National Park in 1872.

_____ **10.** According to this schedule, the new computers *will arrive* tomorrow.

_____ **11.** Jan *had spent* the week at her aunt's house.

_____ **12.** By this time tomorrow, I *will have finished* these tests.

_____ **13.** Stephen usually *rides* to school with us.

_____ **14.** Our pitcher *has won* the game for our team.

_____ **15.** Who *will be* here to help us in the morning?

_____ **16.** The last of the shipment of new books *has arrived*.

_____ **17.** Kerry *rang* the bell at the front gate.

_____ **18.** Our group *will need* a van for the class trip.

_____ **19.** Latoya *seems* happy with her new bicycle.

_____ **20.** On Friday, they *had painted* the stairs leading to the basement.

_____ **21.** For the next meeting, Molly *has agreed* to bring extra notepads.

_____ **22.** We *will have visited* three museums by the end of the day.

_____ **23.** Don, Marie, and I *brought* lettuce, tomatoes, and onions for the salad.

_____ **24.** We *had* never *heard* a bird make such strange noises.

_____ **25.** The committee *has given* this issue a great deal of thought.

LANGUAGE HANDBOOK 3 USING VERBS

| WORKSHEET 8 | **Using Different Verb Tenses**

EXERCISE On the lines provided, rewrite each of the following sentences using the tense shown in parentheses.

> EXAMPLE 1. Marika never sang more beautifully. (*present perfect*)
> _Marika has never sung more beautifully._

1. The bus will leave without us. (*past*) _____

_____

2. Dad wanted you to help with the cooking. (*present*) _____

_____

3. The puppy hurt its right front paw. (*past perfect*) _____

_____

_____

4. Kim made Vietnamese spring rolls for lunch. (*present perfect*) ___

_____

5. After practice, Roscoe and I walk home together. (*future*) _____

_____

_____

6. I finished most of my chores before lunch. (*future perfect*) _____

_____

_____

7. Each morning Julian practiced his free throws and layups. (*present)* __

_____

8. The architect will use a computer to design the museum. (*past*) __

_____

_____

9. Justin read several poems by Ogden Nash. (*present perfect*) _____

_____

_____

10. The gardener planted small bushes along the sidewalk. (*future*) __

_____

_____

LANGUAGE HANDBOOK 3 USING VERBS

WORKSHEET 9 | Using Different Verb Tenses

EXERCISE On the lines provided, rewrite each of the following sentences using the tense shown in parentheses.

> EXAMPLE **1.** Tracy looks forward to trying the potter's wheel. (*past perfect*) _Tracy had looked forward to trying the potter's_ _wheel._

1. We will decorate the gym for the dance. (*past*) _____

_____

2. I sent you a postcard from New York. (*future*) _____

_____

3. My grandparents call me on my birthday. (*future*) _____

_____

4. Several of the lightbulbs burned out. (*present perfect*) _____

_____

5. The gifted storyteller has told the children a Hopi myth. (*past*) _____

_____

_____

6. Erica finished raking the leaves before sundown. (*future perfect*) _____

_____

_____

7. The plumber connected the pipes carefully. (*past perfect*) _____

_____

_____

8. Mr. Foster showed me a painting by John Biggers. (*past perfect*) _____

_____

_____

9. Aunt Marlene repaired the brakes on my bike. (*present perfect*) _____

_____

_____

10. Tourists bought Cuban sandwiches at stands in Little Havana. (*present*) _____

_____

LANGUAGE HANDBOOK **3** USING VERBS

| WORKSHEET 10 | Test

EXERCISE A On the lines provided, write the past tense and the past participle forms of each of the following verbs.

	PAST		PAST PARTICIPLE
EXAMPLE 1. wear	_wore_	(have)	_worn_
1. choose	_____	(have)	_____
2. blow	_____	(have)	_____
3. call	_____	(have)	_____
4. drink	_____	(have)	_____
5. sing	_____	(have)	_____
6. take	_____	(have)	_____
7. dance	_____	(have)	_____
8. give	_____	(have)	_____
9. run	_____	(have)	_____
10. skate	_____	(have)	_____
11. begin	_____	(have)	_____
12. bring	_____	(have)	_____
13. drive	_____	(have)	_____
14. talk	_____	(have)	_____
15. eat	_____	(have)	_____
16. do	_____	(have)	_____
17. fall	_____	(have)	_____
18. steal	_____	(have)	_____
19. write	_____	(have)	_____
20. freeze	_____	(have)	_____

EXERCISE B Underline the correct verb in parentheses in each of the following sentences.

EXAMPLE 1. We (_saw_, seen) a bear the other day.

1. Ingrid and I have often (_rode, ridden_) the bus to school.

2. In a few moments, every balloon had (_burst, bursted_).

Continued ☞

3. Don't (*sit, set*) those bags on the counter; it's wet.

4. Have the exchange students from Wales (*come, came*) to visit yet?

5. Everyone but me has (*knew, known*) about the surprise party.

6. Yori had always (*shrank, shrunk*) from public speaking.

7. Will you (*rise, raise*) the flag this morning?

8. Have you (*went, gone*) to the movies again?

9. The sun had (*rose, risen*) before the plane landed in Sri Lanka.

10. (*Lie, Lay*) down on the sofa until dinnertime.

EXERCISE C On the line provided, write the correct form of the verb given before each sentence.

> **EXAMPLE 1.** *set* He always _____*sets*_____ the pace for the class.

1. *raise*   Peruvian Indians have _____ quinoa, which is a grain, for many centuries.

2. *sit*   Why are you _____ there in the dark?

3. *rise*   As soon as the moon had _____, we set up the telescope.

4. *lay*   Last night, Mom really _____ down the law.

5. *lie*   Your books are _____ all over the floor.

EXERCISE D In the following paragraph, write the correct verb form on the line following each verb in parentheses.

> **EXAMPLE** Yesterday afternoon, Maria [1] (*walk*) _____*walked*_____ home from school.

One afternoon last summer, my brother Jamal and I had [1] (*jog*) _____ around

the park. When we [2] (*come*) _____ home, we were very thirsty. We [3] (*see*)

_____ a bottle of apple juice in the cabinet. We [4] (*take*) _____ the bottle and

[5] (*set*) _____ it in the freezer. Then, we [6] (*lie*) _____ on the air-conditioned

porch. An hour later, we [7] (*go*) _____ to the freezer to get our juice. The bottle

had [8] (*freeze*) _____ and had burst into a million pieces. We should have

[9] (*know*) _____ better. Instead of cold apple juice, we [10] (*drink*) _____

warm tap water while we cleaned up the mess.

WORKSHEET 1   Using Pronouns as Subjects

EXERCISE A   In the following sentences, underline the correct pronoun or pronouns in parentheses.

EXAMPLE **1.** Mr. Reynolds and (_he_, him) led the parade.

1. (*She and I, Her and me*) do not have time for your foolishness.

2. Nina and (*he, him*) could help us.

3. Neither Lani nor (*I, me*) want to miss our morning oatmeal.

4. Jerome and (*they, them*) can name every state.

5. My brother Nicholas and (*she, her*) both want to study Latin next year.

6. After class, (*he and I, him and me*) are going to the bookstore in the mall.

7. Vinnie and (*I, me*) do not go to dances.

8. (*We, Us*) must practice every day for the big competition.

9. (*Her, She*) or Mrs. Stamos will teach history.

10. Should Linda and (*me, I*) learn German folk dancing?

EXERCISE B   On the line provided, write an appropriate pronoun for each of the following sentences. Use a variety of pronouns. Do not use *you* or *it*.

EXAMPLES **1.** On the cliffs, the ranger and ___she___ saw a cougar's den.

2. Have Len and ___he___ set out enough plates for everyone?

1. Olivia and _____ have tried an Indian dish called *matar paneer*.

2. Ali and _____ took their places in line.

3. Are Betty and _____ finished with my dictionary?

4. Mom and _____ are very pleased with their new golf clubs.

5. The principal and _____ greeted the new students.

6. My cousin and _____ are good friends.

7. _____ are choosing a new captain for the track team.

8. Shouldn't you and _____ have brought your books to class?

9. Don't you and _____ leave your books in the living room.

10. _____ enjoyed the soccer match between Italy and Brazil.

LANGUAGE HANDBOOK 4   USING PRONOUNS

| WORKSHEET 2 | Using Pronouns as Predicate Nominatives |

EXERCISE A   Underline the correct pronoun in parentheses in each of the following sentences.

EXAMPLE **1.** The secretary will be Tomás or (*her*, *she*).

1. Our librarian has always been (*him*, *he*).

2. The last ones to board the bus to Canada were the driver and (*us*, *we*).

3. It was (*they*, *them*) who sailed vast distances across the Pacific.

4. Usually, the first ones there are you and (*I*, *me*).

5. Next time, the winners will be (*we*, *us*).

6. The current champions are (*them*, *they*).

7. The girl who speaks Hindi may be (*she*, *her*).

8. Three times last year, the leader in the races was (*me*, *I*).

9. The best catchers on the team are Mindy and (*he*, *him*).

10. The next student council representative will be (*her*, *she*).

EXERCISE B   For each of the following sentences, write an appropriate pronoun on the line provided. Use a variety of pronouns. Do not use *it* or *you*.

EXAMPLES **1.** Was the person at the door ___*he*___?

2. The students with the winning science project were ___*they*___.

1. Could the winner of the trophy be _____?

2. The friendliest of the three boys is _____.

3. The man visiting from Argentina is _____.

4. The woman in the car may be _____.

5. The first-string choices are _____ and your sister.

6. The new student council member is _____.

7. The only twins in school are _____.

8. Your new tennis partner is _____.

9. This fall, our exchange students are Kito and _____.

10. My best friends are my mom and _____.

LANGUAGE HANDBOOK 4 USING PRONOUNS

WORKSHEET 3 | **Using Pronouns as Direct Objects and Indirect Objects**

EXERCISE A   In each of the following sentences, underline the correct pronoun in parentheses.

EXAMPLE 1. The diagrams for the radio puzzled Dad and (*I*, *me*).

1. The Bedouin rider spotted (*he*, *him*) at the oasis.

2. Grandma read (*we*, *us*) her story about coming to Wyoming.

3. A huge stone door shut (*them*, *they*) and (*me*, *I*) inside the courtyard of the castle.

4. My little brother sang (*them*, *they*) a song from nursery school.

5. Nora told Tito and (*she*, *her*) about the change in plans.

6. Sarah's dad showed (*us*, *we*) his cement plant.

7. The bus took Jerome and (*him*, *he*) to the wrong street.

8. A few phone calls saved (*her*, *she*) and (*I*, *me*) a lot of time and money.

9. The sights of Thailand fascinated (*they*, *them*) and (*me*, *I*).

10. Mr. Hernandez asked Lou and (*her*, *she*) for help.

EXERCISE B   Complete each sentence by writing an appropriate pronoun on the line provided. Use a variety of pronouns. Do not use *it* or *you*.

EXAMPLE 1. Can you show Sally and ____*me*____ our mistake?

1. The lieutenant gave the sergeant and _____ weekend passes.

2. Can you tell _____ who Balboa was?

3. Unfortunately, his new jacket does not fit _____ or his brother.

4. The innkeeper showed _____ to our rooms.

5. Cora poured the cat and _____ some milk.

6. Gina helped _____ with the gardening.

7. Please give the forest ranger and _____ these supplies.

8. Someone asked _____ for directions.

9. Will you take the children and _____ home?

10. Angela promised my cousins and _____ a turn on the trampoline.

LANGUAGE HANDBOOK **4** **USING PRONOUNS**

| WORSHEET 4 | **Using Pronouns as Objects of Prepositions** |

EXERCISE A   Circle the preposition in each of the following sentences. Then, underline the correct pronoun in parentheses.

> **EXAMPLE 1.** The puppy ran (after) Joel and (*I, me*).

1. The whole class except (*she, her*) and (*I, me*) visited the museum.

2. This weekend, our team will play against the Cougars and (*they, them*).

3. Hassan explained to (*us, we*) that the Arabs developed algebra.

4. Is this package for you or (*him, he*)?

5. She dropped the puzzle by (*she, her*) and (*I, me*).

6. Is there a genius among (*we, us*)?

7. Zahur told me about (*he, him*).

8. The dog can ride between Ana and (*I, me*).

9. Without (*her, she*), we can't play our best game.

10. This plan is between you and (*I, me*).

EXERCISE B   For each of the following sentences, on the line provided, write a suitable compound object of the italicized preposition. Make at least one part of each object a pronoun.

> **EXAMPLE 1.** Are they talking *about* *Jessie and me* ?

1. The bus just went right *past* _____.

2. She called, and the kitten came *toward* _____.

3. *Like* _____, I practice guitar every evening.

4. The photos of Japan were taken *by* _____.

5. Of course you may sit *beside* _____.

6. All the students *except* _____ must report to the library.

7. We left *without* _____.

8. Just *between* _____, that stew is too spicy.

9. This present is *from* _____.

10. We sat *near* _____ at our favorite Korean restaurant.

NAME _____ CLASS _____ DATE _____

LANGUAGE HANDBOOK **4** USING PRONOUNS

WORKSHEET 5 | Special Pronoun Problems

EXERCISE A Underline the correct pronoun in parentheses in each of the following sentences.

EXAMPLE 1. (*Who*, *Whom*) is the author of *The Land I Lost*?

1. For (*who, whom*) did you write this poem?
2. (*Who, Whom*) has read the story "Everyday Use"?
3. (*Who, Whom*) did you take to the chili festival?
4. To (*who, whom*) did Carlos pass the football?
5. (*Who, Whom*) knows the location of the Amazon River?
6. (*Who, Whom*) was the winner of the marathon?
7. (*Who, Whom*) has Dennis invited to the party?
8. (*Who, Whom*) will make posters for the crafts fair?
9. (*Who, Whom*) is your new neighbor?
10. (*Who, Whom*) did Jason sit with at the softball game?

EXERCISE B Underline the correct pronoun in parentheses in each of the following sentences.

EXAMPLE 1. (*We*, *Us*) members of the nature club are organizing a fund-raiser.

1. The first ones on stage were (*we, us*) acrobats.
2. Friday evening (*we, us*) girls watched a movie starring Anthony Quinn.
3. Mr. Pierce showed (*we, us*) students a carved wooden doll called a kachina.
4. Coach Hena gave (*we, us*) hockey players a good pep talk.
5. Grandfather made bean burritos for (*we, us*) grandchildren and our friends.
6. (*We, Us*) drummers have been rehearsing two hours a day.
7. The winners of the game will be (*we, us*) Hawks.
8. Why didn't you tell (*we, us*) student council members about the problem?
9. Mrs. Sato took (*we, us*) class members on a field trip to the state capitol.
10. All of (*we, us*) track athletes admire Jackie Joyner-Kersee.

| LANGUAGE HANDBOOK | **4** | **USING PRONOUNS** |

| **WORKSHEET 6** | Test |

EXERCISE A   Identify the following pronouns as subject forms, object forms, or possessive forms. On the line provided, write *S* if a pronoun is a subject form, *O* if a pronoun is an object form, or *P* if a pronoun is a possessive form. If a pronoun can be both a subject form and an object form, write *S/O*. If a pronoun can be both an object form and a possessive form, write *O/P*.

EXAMPLE ___*S/O*___ **1.** it

_____ **1.** us   _____ **11.** its

_____ **2.** yours   _____ **12.** me

_____ **3.** he   _____ **13.** my

_____ **4.** they   _____ **14.** her

_____ **5.** our   _____ **15.** your

_____ **6.** him   _____ **16.** mine

_____ **7.** them   _____ **17.** his

_____ **8.** we   _____ **18.** you

_____ **9.** she   _____ **19.** I

_____ **10.** theirs   _____ **20.** hers

EXERCISE B   On the line provided, write the subject form of a pronoun to complete each of the following sentences. Use a variety of pronouns, but do not use *you* or *it*.

EXAMPLE **1.** ___*I*___ really enjoyed the film about seals.

1. The only girl on the team was _____.

2. Luckily, Mario and _____ own a bicycle pump.

3. _____ cautiously approached the strange dog.

4. Are _____ really going to place a call to Akio's brother in Japan?

5. The umpire at our games is _____.

6. Is _____ going to play the lead in our school play?

7. Sarah's father and _____ are going to the state fair.

8. The two best tennis players are _____ and _____.

9. _____ opened the cupboard and took out a can of soup.

10. Jessica and _____ have three cats.

Continued ☞

LANGUAGE HANDBOOK 4 WORKSHEET 6 (continued)

EXERCISE C   On the line provided, write the object form of a pronoun to complete each of the following sentences. Use a variety of pronouns, but do not use *you* or *it*.

EXAMPLE **1.** Is this message on the table for ___*her*___ or you?

1. Did you ask _____ your question?

2. I saved you and _____ tickets for the concert.

3. The gentleman beside _____ is the mayor's secretary.

4. Call _____ after the announcement.

5. A computer can tell _____ the answer to our question.

6. Mrs. Kolar gave Marcia and _____ a special project.

7. Has anyone told _____ when the movie starts?

8. I did not notice _____ at the game.

9. Ask _____ what spices to put in the sauce.

10. The bookshelf behind _____ holds a set of encyclopedias.

EXERCISE D   On the line provided, identify the form of each italicized pronoun as *S* for subject or *O* for object.

EXAMPLES ___*S*___ **1.** The captain of our basketball team is *she*.

___*O*___ **2.** They asked the police officer to give *them* directions to the nearest gas station.

_____ **1.** Tell *her* about Norwegian explorer Roald Amundsen.

_____ **2.** Did *he* draw the picture on the board?

_____ **3.** Ms. Nichols taught *them* the basics of gymnastics.

_____ **4.** Van and *she* will bring the paper cups.

_____ **5.** The dentist showed the X-rays to *me*.

_____ **6.** Both Carl and *he* help to manage the bookstore.

_____ **7.** The rake you need is next to *her*.

_____ **8.** Unless you tell them, *they* won't know which way to go.

_____ **9.** The person who brought the tape player was *I*.

_____ **10.** Did you ask *him* where he put it?

Continued ☞

EXERCISE E   In the proper column below, write the corresponding form of the given personal pronoun.

	SUBJECT	OBJECT
EXAMPLE 1.	I	me
1.	we	_____
2.	_____	him
3.	_____	them
4.	she	_____
5.	they	_____

EXERCISE F   In each of the following sentences, underline the correct pronoun in parentheses.

EXAMPLE 1. Sue and (*I, me*) tossed the horseshoes a little too hard.

1. Dad has a surprise for Mom and (*us, we*).

2. Would you tell Dana and (*I, me*) about your trip to France?

3. The new Scout leader for our troop will be Etta or (*her, she*).

4. The winners were (*us, we*) Falcons.

5. Leon and (*them, they*) made a mobile for the baby's crib.

6. Watch your brother and (*he, him*) this afternoon.

7. Please, take the seat between Pilar and (*he, him*).

8. Did you tell Gramps and (*her, she*) the news?

9. In the kitchen were my uncles and (*her, she*).

10. The librarian handed Marco and (*he, him*) two books about Kenya.

EXERCISE G   In each of the following sentences, underline the correct pronoun in parentheses.

EXAMPLE 1. Could the man in the green car have been (*he, him*)?

1. Ms. O'Brien explained to (*we, us*) that Matthew Henson was among the first people to reach the North Pole.

2. Would you draw a map for (*them, they*) and their friends?

3. Monica showed Dad and (*him, he*) her award for the science fair project.

Continued ☞

4. Otis and (*I, me*) will go with Uncle Van to the concert.

5. Mrs. Moskowitz and (*she, her*) enjoy a good joke.

6. Will that man be taking a picture of the team and (*us, we*)?

7. Zach and (*me, I*) don't like reptiles very much.

8. The canals in Venice, Italy, impressed (*they, them*).

9. Broad fields of flowers delighted the tourists and (*her, she*).

10. (*We, Us*) English students aren't scared by grammar.

EXERCISE H   If a pronoun is used incorrectly in the following sentences, draw a line through it. Then, on the line provided, write the correct pronoun. If a sentence is already correct, write *C*.

EXAMPLE ___they___ **1.** Don't ~~them~~ care about our feelings?

_____ **1.** My Dad and me like to listen to the music of Louis Armstrong.

_____ **2.** Us sports fans like a close game best of all.

_____ **3.** When is the surprise party for her and him?

_____ **4.** The magician chose Mario and she for his next trick.

_____ **5.** Just keep this a secret between you and I.

_____ **6.** The Brazilian carnival masks were worn by them.

_____ **7.** The pilot showed my mom and I the jet's instrument panel.

_____ **8.** My sister and she share a bedroom in our condo.

_____ **9.** All the cousins except you and her are good at puzzles.

_____ **10.** Did you give Boris and he our new fax number?

_____ **11.** David and me repaired the latch on the gate.

_____ **12.** We gave Sharla and they four tickets to the basketball game.

_____ **13.** The holiday brought a much-needed break to we students.

_____ **14.** Last night, Barry and her finished their homework quickly.

_____ **15.** The judge presented Jim and she with first prize for the best math project.

_____ **16.** He and them spoke to our writing group.

_____ **17.** Could we sit over there next to Barbara and she?

_____ **18.** All at once, Denise and him turned and ran up the stairs.

_____ **19.** How many students voted for you and he instead of the other team?

_____ **20.** Tomorrow, us members of the history club will meet at city hall.

Continued ☞

EXERCISE I   In each of the following sentences, underline the correct pronoun in parentheses.

> EXAMPLE 1. (<u>Who</u>, Whom) has already bought the new Whitney Houston CD?

1. To (*who, whom*) did your aunt send birth announcements?
2. (*Who, Whom*) is the owner of this beautiful Irish setter?
3. If it is raining, (*who, whom*) will drive us to the theater?
4. (*Who, Whom*) did you see at the powwow?
5. With (*who, whom*) did Mario study for the science test?
6. (*Who, Whom*) would like a set of chopsticks?
7. (*Who, Whom*) was the soloist at last night's concert?
8. (*Who, Whom*) will the class choose as spokesperson?
9. (*Who, Whom*) plays the part of the villain in that movie?
10. (*Who, Whom*) have you talked to about the plans?

EXERCISE J   In each of the following sentences, underline the correct pronoun in parentheses.

> EXAMPLE 1. Please give (*we, <u>us</u>*) hikers a map of the area.

1. (*We, Us*) golfers have improved with the help of Coach Jackson.
2. Mrs. Levin talked to (*we, us*) clarinet players before band practice.
3. Aunt Sara asked (*we, us*) children for some help with her garden.
4. The Scout leader handed (*we, us*) campers first-aid kits.
5. At the planetarium (*we, us*) students quietly took our seats.
6. The winners of the tournament are (*we, us*) Cougars.
7. Mother read (*we, us*) girls a poem by Nikki Giovanni.
8. Uncle Dwayne drove (*we, us*) children to the game.
9. Mr. Newman demonstrated the conga, a Cuban dance, for (*we, us*) students.
10. The first people to jump into the swimming pool were (*we, us*) three boys.

LANGUAGE HANDBOOK **5** USING MODIFIERS

WORKSHEET 1 Understanding the Comparison of Adjectives and Adverbs

EXERCISE A   In the proper column below, write the comparative and superlative forms of the following adjectives.

POSITIVE	COMPARATIVE	SUPERLATIVE
EXAMPLES 1. wet	*wetter*	*wettest*
2. difficult	*more difficult*	*most difficult*
1. low	_____	_____
2. enjoyable	_____	_____
3. safe	_____	_____
4. cowardly	_____	_____
5. strange	_____	_____
6. sharp	_____	_____
7. clean	_____	_____
8. foolishly	_____	_____
9. quick	_____	_____
10. dangerous	_____	_____

EXERCISE B   On the line provided, write the correct comparative or superlative form of the word in italics.

EXAMPLE 1. *fast* Only the _____ *fastest* _____ runner in the school will race at the meet.

1. *pleasant* That day was the _____ day of our vacation.

2. *strong* Is a yak _____ than a water buffalo?

3. *wildly* The bronco bucked _____ today than it did yesterday.

4. *warm* This is the _____ blanket in the closet.

5. *brave* Of the two warriors, Xena is the _____.

6. *quickly* Tara responded _____ than Paul did.

7. *high* Mount Everest is the _____ mountain in the world.

8. *happily* The children laughed _____ than they had all month.

9. *dark* Last night may have been the _____ night of the year.

10. *good* That salad was _____ than the last one.

LANGUAGE HANDBOOK **5**	**USING MODIFIERS**

WORKSHEET 2 | Using *Good* and *Well*

EXERCISE A   In each of the following sentences, underline the correct modifier in parentheses.

> **EXAMPLES** 1. You played the part very (*good*, <u>*well*</u>).
>
> 2. We knew that you would do a (<u>*good*</u>, *well*) job.

1. Do you know Persian (*well*, *good*) enough to translate for us?

2. For once, your bedroom looks (*good*, *well*)!

3. These pears taste (*well*, *good*).

4. Many people can speak two languages equally (*good*, *well*).

5. A little exercise would be (*well*, *good*) for you.

6. The puppy does not feel (*good*, *well*), so we are taking him to the vet.

7. Roses do not grow (*well*, *good*) for me.

8. What smells so (*good*, *well*) in the kitchen?

9. The plan sounds (*well*, *good*) to me.

10. Our trip to Mexico started badly, but it ended (*good*, *well*).

EXERCISE B   On each line provided, write the correct form of either *good* or *well*.

> **EXAMPLES** 1. I did ___*well*___ on the math quiz.
>
> 2. She did __*better*__ than I did on the quiz.

1. You speak Italian quite _____.

2. In time, Carla became _____ at computer programming than I was.

3. How _____ are you at adding numbers in your head?

4. Do a _____ job labeling your map of South America than you did yesterday.

5. Sweep the floor, and then scrub it _____.

6. Of all my classes, I like science _____.

7. These crackers are _____, but those are better.

8. Of the two men, the older was the _____ writer.

9. She plays the guitar very _____.

10. This is the _____ banana in the bunch.

LANGUAGE HANDBOOK **5** USING MODIFIERS

WORKSHEET 3 ## Using Irregular Comparisons; Avoiding Double Comparisons

EXERCISE A On the line provided, write the correct form of the word in italics.

EXAMPLE **1.** *good* This party is the _____*best*_____ one ever!

1. *well* Kelly, you certainly draw horses _____ than I do.

2. *good* A green salad tastes _____ with dinner than it does by itself.

3. *many* Who had the _____ points in the spelling bee?

4. *bad* Lelani's jokes are _____ than mine.

5. *much* We have _____ time to fish today than we had yesterday.

6. *well* Of all the members of my family, I do the chores _____.

7. *many* That store offers _____ choices than the one down the street.

8. *good* Your revised paragraph about Antarctica is _____ than the original one.

9. *far* My group went _____ than the other groups.

10. *bad* Will the weather be _____ tomorrow than it is today?

EXERCISE B Draw a line through each incorrect modifier in the following sentences. Then, on the line provided, write the correct modifier. If a sentence is already correct, write *C*.

EXAMPLES _____*better*_____ **1.** That movie is ~~more better~~ than this one.

_____*C*_____ **2.** Unfortunately, she is feeling worse today.

_____ **1.** Of all the trees, this eucalyptus has been hurt worse by the freeze.

_____ **2.** This model is the more better one in your collection.

_____ **3.** Between you and me, I have the mostest marbles.

_____ **4.** Did you see many koalas on your trip to Australia?

_____ **5.** Of the four brands of pita bread, this one tastes better.

_____ **6.** The car is running more worse now than it was before.

_____ **7.** Of the two shirts, the yellow one looks best on you.

_____ **8.** Well, this meal is better than your last one.

_____ **9.** Of the two books, the one about the Amazon is best.

_____ **10.** That was the worst thing that could have happened to us.

| WORKSHEET 4 | ## Avoiding Double Comparisons and Double Negatives |

EXERCISE A   Some of the following sentences contain a double comparison. Draw a line through any incorrect modifiers. Then, on the line provided, write the correct form. If a sentence is already correct, write *C*.

EXAMPLE ____*loveliest*____ **1.** That is the ~~most loveliest~~ tree on the street.

_____ **1.** That rug has made your room much more cozier than it was before.

_____ **2.** Ashur's never seen anything more taller than Mount Everest.

_____ **3.** Watch out! That's the most worst dog in the world.

_____ **4.** Is your mother feeling more better today than she was Monday?

_____ **5.** I don't have the money for a more expensive watch.

_____ **6.** Chile's Atacama Desert is one of the most driest regions in the world.

_____ **7.** That horse is acting even more strangely today than it was yesterday.

_____ **8.** The crowd had never seen a more stronger wrestler than this one.

_____ **9.** This knife is the most sharpest one on the rack.

_____ **10.** We can cross the stream more safely at the bridge than at the ford.

EXERCISE B   Draw a line through any double negatives in the following sentences. Then, on the line provided, write the correct form.

EXAMPLE ___*didn't hear anything*___ **1.** We ~~didn't hear nothing~~ about the dance.

_____ **1.** There isn't nobody in my class from my old school.

_____ **2.** Jade doesn't tell us barely anything about her work.

_____ **3.** Haven't you never read about the ancient country of Phoenicia?

_____ **4.** Don't you hardly know better than that?

_____ **5.** I won't take none of your oranges.

_____ **6.** Hard work won't hurt nobody.

_____ **7.** I can't see nothing from here.

_____ **8.** You don't have no stories about Iceland, do you?

_____ **9.** Lucia didn't say nothing about you or your friends.

_____ **10.** Don't you never go out in those woods alone!

LANGUAGE HANDBOOK 5 USING MODIFIERS

| WORKSHEET 5 | Test

EXERCISE A   On the line provided, write the correct comparative or superlative form of the word in italics before each of the following sentences.

> EXAMPLE 1. *big* Don't take the ____biggest____ of the three apples.

1. *easy*   The Silk Road to China was not exactly the _____ route to travel.

2. *strong*   Only the _____ animals survive these winters.

3. *quickly*   Can't you walk _____ than that?

4. *slow*   This must be the _____ bus in the world.

5. *kind*   I don't know of a _____ person than Mr. Franklin.

6. *old*   This oak is the _____ tree in the whole county.

7. *carefully* Read the instructions _____ than the last time.

8. *difficult* The last chapter of the book was the _____.

9. *loudly*   He plays steel drum music _____ than I do.

10. *frequently* Brush your teeth _____ than you do now, and you won't need to go to the dentist so often.

EXERCISE B   On the line provided, write the correct comparative or superlative form of the word in italics before each of the following sentences.

> EXAMPLE 1. *bad* This bunch of grapes is ____worse____ than the last one.

1. *far*   Inés walked _____ than anyone else as we explored the streets of Montreal.

2. *much*   Does anyone have _____ fun than we do?

3. *good*   Frank has the _____ science project in the school.

4. *well*   I never could sing _____ than my sister.

5. *bad*   Because of frequent natural disasters, Bangladesh is one of the _____ places to live.

6. *much*   Which nation produces the _____ cotton?

7. *well*   Few animals can hunt _____ than a jaguar.

8. *many*   The southern states have the _____ storms.

9. *good*   Our new computer has _____ programs than the old one.

10. *bad*   Don't worry; you won't be the _____ dancer on the floor.

Continued ☞

LANGUAGE HANDBOOK **5** **WORSHEET 5** (continued)

EXERCISE C   On the line provided in each of the following sentences, write either *good* or *well*.

EXAMPLE **1.** This heater has not been working ___well___ all winter.

1. She always performs _____ in a race.

2. Alicia can golf as _____ as her father.

3. The Sahel region of Africa is not a _____ place to grow crops.

4. The rest of the melon appears _____ to me.

5. You look pale; don't you feel _____?

EXERCISE D   In each of the following sentences, underline the correct word in parentheses.

EXAMPLE **1.** My old coat will not fit me (*any more*, *no more*).

1. Don't do (*nothing*, *anything*) you will regret later.

2. Randy (*shouldn't never have*, *should never have*) tried to throw that pass.

3. Hasn't (*anybody*, *nobody*) arrived yet to unlock the doors?

4. After dinner, neither of my brothers was (*anywhere*, *nowhere*) to be found.

5. We scarcely (*never*, *ever*) watch television on school nights.

EXERCISE E   Draw a line through each incorrect modifier in the following sentences. Then, write the correct form on the line provided. If a sentence is already correct, write *C*.

EXAMPLE ___any___ **1.** This isn't the place for no foolishness.

_____ **1.** Bollywood, the world's most largest film industry, is located in Bombay, India.

_____ **2.** Isn't this the most scariest movie that you've ever seen?

_____ **3.** Those reflectors look good on your bicycle.

_____ **4.** There's hardly nothing for teenagers to do in this town.

_____ **5.** She has the bestest luck of anyone I know.

_____ **6.** That outfit looks even worser than the first one.

_____ **7.** Wow! You can really throw good.

_____ **8.** Don't let none of the cattle into the rice paddy.

_____ **9.** An athlete doesn't never stop training.

_____ **10.** I've never seen a more beautiful day than today.

NAME _____ CLASS _____ DATE _____

LANGUAGE HANDBOOK **6** **THE PREPOSITIONAL PHRASE**

| WORKSHEET 1 | **Identifying and Using Prepositional Phrases**

EXERCISE A Each of the following sentences contains a prepositional phrase. Underline the preposition. Then, circle the object or objects of the preposition.

> **EXAMPLE 1.** Letters <u>without</u> a (stamp) and an (address) will not be delivered.

1. Andrei Ivanov rafted down the Oygaing River.

2. The pizza shop is having a dinner special on Wednesday evening.

3. The St. Lawrence River empties into the Atlantic Ocean.

4. Did you look under the bed and the sofa?

5. Be quiet during the lecture.

6. The man across the street makes beautiful guitars and violins.

7. Bright sunshine streamed through the windows and the open door.

8. Will the announcement be made by Mr. Cohen or Ms. Turner?

9. The Inuit came from Greenland and Siberia.

10. Nana told us a story about her aunt and uncle.

EXERCISE B Complete each of the following sentences by writing an appropriate prepositional phrase on the line provided. Do not use the same prepositional phrase twice.

> **EXAMPLE 1.** The mountains ____of Tibet____ are covered with snow.

1. That screwdriver _____ is mine.

2. Aunt Beth lives _____.

3. Take this letter _____.

4. Your books and your jacket are still _____.

5. Did you see the movie _____?

6. Your bike is leaning _____.

7. Please carry the groceries _____.

8. Is the band going to play _____?

9. The tomatoes _____ must be washed.

10. _____, we are going on a picnic.

LANGUAGE HANDBOOK 6 THE PREPOSITIONAL PHRASE

WORKSHEET 2 | **Identifying and Using Adjective Phrases**

EXERCISE A Underline each adjective phrase in the following sentences. Then, draw an arrow from the phrase to the word it modifies. Some sentences contain more than one adjective phrase.

EXAMPLE 1. The hallway in the house was dark and scary.

1. The fleur-de-lis is a symbol of independence.

2. All CDs for the computer should be put away.

3. The first player through the door carried the lacrosse trophy.

4. Astronomers study the positions of stars and planets.

5. The girls on the track team may leave now.

6. Mr. Lee showed a film about thunder and lightning.

7. Choose a reliable product with a good price.

8. Islam is the chief religion of the Middle East.

9. A woman at the front door is selling brushes for dogs.

10. They questioned every passenger aboard the ship.

EXERCISE B On the line provided, write a suitable adjective phrase for each of the following sentences. Do not use the same phrase twice.

EXAMPLE 1. A sudden rain caused the cancellation of the art show
_____at the lake_____.

1. Large signs in the window _____ announced the sale.

2. Cocker spaniels are a breed _____ that many people favor as pets.

3. Only one flower _____ was still unopened.

4. The park _____ has a special zoo for baby animals.

5. Aunt Cara gave me a book _____.

6. We startled a flock _____.

7. Tests showed a great improvement _____.

8. A letter _____ came only this morning.

9. Tickets for the concert _____ will be available soon.

10. The myths _____ are still well known.

LANGUAGE HANDBOOK **6** THE PREPOSITIONAL PHRASE

WORKSHEET 3 | Using Adverb Phrases

EXERCISE A   Underline each adverb phrase in the following sentences. Then, draw an arrow from the phrase to the word or words that it modifies. A sentence may contain more than one adverb phrase.

> **EXAMPLE 1.** We are leaving <u>on Saturday</u> <u>at dawn</u>.

1. The kitten dashed around the room.

2. Rain splattered our clothes with mud and dripped into our shoes.

3. Warsaw, Poland, is located on the Vistula River.

4. I never leave my bicycle on the lawn.

5. You may watch television after dinner for an hour.

6. A bright lamp shone beside the leather chair.

7. We drove around the block several times.

8. The Incas of South America lived in the Andes Mountains.

9. During the night, burglars crept into the bank.

10. Do not throw that log on the fire!

EXERCISE B   On each line provided, write a sentence that contains the given prepositional phrase used as an adverb phrase.

> **EXAMPLE 1.** to my mother _This book belongs to my mother._

1. in Spanish-speaking countries _____

2. in the basement _____

3. beside the washer _____

4. along the path _____

5. toward school _____

6. during the day _____

7. into the water _____

8. at three o'clock _____

9. down the hill _____

10. in China _____

LANGUAGE HANDBOOK 6 THE PREPOSITIONAL PHRASE

WORKSHEET 4 ## Distinguishing Between Adjective Phrases and Adverb Phrases

EXERCISE A   Underline each prepositional phrase in the following sentences. Draw an arrow from the phrase to the word it modifies. Then, on the line provided, identify each phrase as *ADJ* for adjective phrase or *ADV* for adverb phrase.

> EXAMPLE   _ADV, ADV_   **1.** In the morning, my sister and I took the canoe to the river.

_____   **1.** At the tunnel, the train blew its whistle

_____   **2.** The dense fog around us made travel impossible.

_____   **3.** Knowledge of papermaking reached Europe in the twelfth century.

_____   **4.** A score above fourteen points will win this round.

_____   **5.** Guitar music drifted sweetly through the air.

_____   **6.** The current took our raft down the creek.

_____   **7.** Will the questions on the test be difficult?

_____   **8.** Do not use the disks in the green box.

_____   **9.** The poetry of Langston Hughes remains popular.

_____   **10.** The dolphin dived under the water, surfaced, and jumped over the rope.

EXERCISE B   Each of the following sentences contains a phrase in italics. Draw an arrow from the phrase to the word it modifies. Then, on the line provided, identify the phrase in italics as *ADJ* for adjective phrase or *ADV* for adverb phrase.

> EXAMPLE   _ADJ_   **1.** I go to a camp *in the Catskill Mountains*.

_____   **1.** The Ottawa hunted *among the tall trees* near the lake.

_____   **2.** The man *across the street* tossed our football back to us.

_____   **3.** Mirrors reflected the light *from the candle*.

_____   **4.** The stories *on this list* were written by Mary Whitebird.

_____   **5.** The baby rode *in a sling* on Dad's back.

_____   **6.** The cows grazed *on weeds and grass*.

_____   **7.** We waded through a huge drift *of powdery snow*.

_____   **8.** Rivers of lava flowed *from the volcano*.

_____   **9.** People *throughout the world* enjoy a good story.

_____   **10.** Go around the house *to the back door*.

LANGUAGE HANDBOOK **6** THE PREPOSITIONAL PHRASE

WORKSHEET 5 | **Test**

EXERCISE A   Underline the prepositional phrase in each of the following sentences. Then, circle the preposition in each phrase.

EXAMPLES 1. Chris was the next person (at) bat.

2. (During) the game, we cheered our team.

1. Lacrosse is a game invented by North American Indians.

2. Trains at the station must blow their whistles.

3. Sit down and relax for a minute.

4. We played our new computer games until dinner.

5. Corn always grows well in that field.

6. Few mammals can live beyond the Arctic Circle.

7. Ideas without action are not worth much.

8. Hundreds of jellyfish dotted the surf.

9. Mohan picked some wildflowers along the road.

10. Throughout the night, the mariachi band played.

EXERCISE B   Underline the prepositional phrase in each of the following sentences. Then, circle the object or objects of each preposition.

EXAMPLE 1. Mr. Young gave a party for our (class) and his (team).

1. The books were about famous African American inventors and scientists.

2. Our town always has a parade on Saint Patrick's Day.

3. The capital of New Mexico will be our next stop.

4. Was that telephone call for Malini or me?

5. Friends like him are very valuable.

6. Do not disturb them during exam week.

7. All the girls attended except Ruth, Judith, and me.

8. By breakfast time, we had hiked the entire trail.

9. Someday, perhaps, people will travel beyond our solar system.

10. Do we need spices for Irish stew?

Continued ☞

EXERCISE C   Underline the prepositional phrase in each of the following sentences. Then, draw an arrow from the phrase to the word or words that it modifies.

EXAMPLE   **1.** The pencil on the desk is not mine.

1. Otters were sunning themselves on the rocks.

2. You can sit beside Aretha and me.

3. My relatives from Italy arrived today.

4. The reservoir by the Texas-Mexico border is called Amistad.

5. Luckily, I had put my wallet in my pocket.

6. Did you tell Jamal about the game?

7. Several dogs behind the fence jumped up and barked fiercely.

8. Students often meet here between classes.

9. Certain types of fish may not be caught here.

10. The train passed through the Swiss Alps.

EXERCISE D   On the line provided, identify each phrase in italics as *ADJ* for adjective phrase or *ADV* for adverb phrase.

EXAMPLES   __ADJ__   **1.** The spaniel greeted us with barks *of joy*.

__ADV__   **2.** Five inches of rain fell *during the afternoon* and caused Onion Creek to flood.

_____   **1.** Gardens are an important part *of Japanese life and art*.

_____   **2.** The biggest tree *in the county* grows beside the Indian River.

_____   **3.** I have not sailed on a boat *since last July*.

_____   **4.** He repaired the bicycle *with spare parts*.

_____   **5.** We rented an apartment *with a view* of the park.

_____   **6.** Jugglers in costumes *of bright colors* entertained us.

_____   **7.** Spiders ran *along the windows* of the shack.

_____   **8.** This photograph is of Masud's house *near Oakland*.

_____   **9.** A bus leaves *at dawn* for Melbourne, Australia.

_____   **10.** The climb *down this mountain* is very dangerous without proper equipment.

LANGUAGE
HANDBOOK **7** SENTENCES

| WORKSHEET 1 | **Distinguishing Sentences and Sentence Fragments**

EXERCISE Some of the following word groups are sentences, and some are sentence fragments. On the line provided, write *SF* if a word group is a sentence fragment. If a word group is a sentence, rewrite the word group with proper capitalization and punctuation.

EXAMPLES 1. the old car started with a roar *The old car started with a roar.*

2. a saddle for a camel *SF*

1. gently drifted over the calm blue waters _____

_____

2. the jet plane soared out of sight _____

_____

3. spent only part of her allowance _____

_____

4. your dad certainly is in a good mood _____

_____

5. the big gray dog at the end of my block _____

_____

6. my brother read some of the poems of Ricardo Sánchez _____

_____

7. a wonderful day for a walk in the park _____

_____

8. Mohenjo-Daro, a center of the Indus Valley civilization _____

_____

9. a silver trout took the bait _____

_____

10. yellow buses waited at the curb _____

_____

WORKSHEET 2 | **Identifying and Using Complete Subjects and Simple Subjects**

EXERCISE A   Underline the complete subject in each of the following sentences.

EXAMPLE **1.** Under the bushes was <u>a baby rabbit.</u>

1. Josephina walked along the pier to the bait shop.

2. The entire class enjoyed reading Langston Hughes's poems.

3. An astronomer studies stars and their movements.

4. In the suitcase were old photographs of my Irish grandparents.

5. Jean guided us through the museum.

EXERCISE B   Underline the complete subject. Then, on the line provided, write the simple subject.

EXAMPLE _____*music*_____ **1.** <u>Strange, loud music</u> woke us in the night.

_____ **1.** Professor Zhang explained the instructions to us.

_____ **2.** In the top drawer were several keys.

_____ **3.** From the crater flowed hot lava.

_____ **4.** Many types of insects live in this swamp.

_____ **5.** The kitten slept peacefully under the bed.

_____ **6.** Sacagawea was a Shoshone guide.

_____ **7.** The curious raccoon tipped over the table.

_____ **8.** Fluffy chicks ran around the farmyard.

_____ **9.** Beside the window was a chair.

_____ **10.** Nguyen Thi Vinh is a Vietnamese writer best known for her fiction.

EXERCISE C   Add a complete subject to each of the following word groups. Then, circle the simple subject. Do not use the same subject twice.

EXAMPLE **1.** Under the tree were _____(dozens) of acorns._____

1. _____ is my favorite poet.

2. _____ twinkled in the sky above us.

3. On the table was _____.

4. _____ broke into a thousand pieces.

5. _____ shines in my bedroom window.

LANGUAGE HANDBOOK **7** **SENTENCES**

WORSHEET 3 **Identifying Complete Subjects and Predicates**

EXERCISE A   Underline the complete subject in each of the following sentences.

> **EXAMPLE** 1. <u>The whole class</u> studied for the science test.

1. Lori discovered an old trunk in the attic.

2. Ma Rainey was a blues singer.

3. Our tent fell down during the storm.

4. Late in the afternoon, huge white clouds hid the sun.

5. Sleeping in a corner of the cage was a big black snake.

EXERCISE B   Underline the complete predicate in each of the following sentences.

> **EXAMPLE** 1. We <u>stabled the horses for the night</u>.

1. Frederick Douglass is one of many African American heroes.

2. My sister at Gallaudet University gave me a puppy.

3. I bought the concert tickets last week.

4. That sailboat belongs to my father and mother.

5. Caleb told me about the wild animals in Australia.

6. The winners of the soccer championship accepted the trophy.

7. A good driver follows the rules of the road.

8. Good health depends upon proper nutrition.

9. Our grandparents live on the north coast of Africa.

10. Madri's colorful sari shone in the moonlight.

EXERCISE C   On the line provided, add either a complete subject or a complete predicate to each of the following word groups.

> **EXAMPLE** 1. Your library books and your papers *are on the kitchen table.*

1. A sleek, black Arabian mare _____.

2. _____ kicked the soccer ball for another goal.

3. Our new computer with a color printer _____.

4. _____ flew high above our heads.

5. In art class, we made _____.

LANGUAGE HANDBOOK 7 SENTENCES

| WORKSHEET 4 | **Identifying Complete Predicates and Simple Predicates** |

EXERCISE A Underline each complete predicate.

> **EXAMPLES** 1. Elephants <u>played in the wide, cool river</u>.
>
> 2. <u>In the bottom of the laundry basket</u>, I <u>found my shirt</u>.

1. Maria is going to the pep rally.

2. The towering crags of the Teton Range blocked our view of the sun.

3. Across the Great Salt Lake warm breezes swept.

4. I am giving my mother Elie Wiesel's autobiography *Night* for her birthday.

5. In a basket slept three very large Great Dane puppies.

6. Victor answered the question about the Nile River.

7. My father promised me a treehouse.

8. A vast herd of buffalo once thundered across the plains.

9. The bright lights of the streets of New York City welcomed us.

10. Many students in my school speak Vietnamese.

EXERCISE B Underline each complete predicate. Then, write the simple predicate (verb) on the line provided.

> **EXAMPLES** ___decorated___ 1. Swords <u>decorated the walls</u>.
>
> ___Have seen___ 2. <u>Have</u> you <u>seen my glasses</u>?

_____ 1. A golden sunset lights the western sky.

_____ 2. Did someone play a sonata by Beethoven on the piano?

_____ 3. We listened to a recording of Dr. Martin Luther King, Jr.'s famous speech.

_____ 4. Books tell all their secrets to the reader.

_____ 5. Austin, Texas, is home to North America's largest urban colony of bats.

_____ 6. We saw the smoke from their campfire.

_____ 7. The leader of the Lions Club gave a talk about community service projects.

_____ 8. Ernesto lifted the baby out of the crib.

_____ 9. Do you write poetry for enjoyment?

_____ 10. My sister taught me the words to the song.

LANGUAGE HANDBOOK 7 SENTENCES

| WORKSHEET 5 | **Identifying and Using Complete Predicates and Simple Predicates** |

EXERCISE   Add a complete predicate to the following word groups. Then, circle the simple predicate (verb). Do not use the same predicate twice.

EXAMPLE **1.** A dolphin (swims) playfully near our boat. _____

1. My best friend _____
_____

2. Mexico _____
_____

3. A car with a convertible top _____
_____
_____

4. Stacks of lumber _____
_____

5. The shiny, new bicycle _____
_____

6. Our neighbors _____
_____

7. My vacation plans _____
_____

8. The large truck _____
_____

9. The custodian of our school _____
_____

10. My favorite dinner _____
_____

LANGUAGE HANDBOOK 7 SENTENCES

WORKSHEET 6 | Identifying Compound Subjects and Verbs

EXERCISE A   Underline each simple subject in the following sentences. If a sentence has a compound subject, write *CS* for compound subject on the line provided.

EXAMPLE ___*CS*___ 1. A <u>horse</u> and <u>colt</u> grazed on our front lawn.

_____ 1. *Guitar* and *Guernica* are abstract paintings by Pablo Picasso.

_____ 2. My parents promised me a trip to the beach.

_____ 3. Little plants pushed toward the sun and spread their leaves.

_____ 4. With the new century came wonderful discoveries.

_____ 5. Ernest or Raul will return your library books.

_____ 6. Radishes, carrots, and tomatoes are growing in our garden this year.

_____ 7. Senegal is a French-speaking country.

_____ 8. Beatrice left a message for you.

_____ 9. Mighty tigers and elephants roamed the jungles of India.

_____ 10. Squares, circles, and rectangles are geometric forms.

EXERCISE B   Underline the verb or verbs in each of the following sentences. If a sentence has a compound verb, write *CV* for compound verb on the line provided.

EXAMPLES ___*CV*___ 1. The Scouts <u>studied</u> birds and <u>drew</u> pictures of them.

___*CV*___ 2. Morgan <u>will wash</u> the potatoes and <u>will slice</u> the carrots.

_____ 1. Her new kite soared through the air but landed in a tree.

_____ 2. Football and basketball require teamwork.

_____ 3. Burkina Faso is located in Western Africa.

_____ 4. The class either reads or practices mathematics during study hall.

_____ 5. Either Hans or Miguel will lead the parade next week.

_____ 6. Many Mexican American writers switch between Spanish and English in their works.

_____ 7. Inger enjoyed the party but left early.

_____ 8. A tall ship sailed into the harbor and docked at the pier.

_____ 9. The Scouts made camp and went on a hike.

_____ 10. Carl and Nola finished the course in record time.

LANGUAGE HANDBOOK **7** **SENTENCES**

WORKSHEET 7 | **Test**

EXERCISE A Each of the following word groups is missing either a subject or a predicate. Add whatever words are necessary to make each word group a complete sentence. Write your sentences on the lines provided. Remember to include proper capitalization and punctuation.

EXAMPLE **1.** the helmet with the red stripes <u>The helmet with the red stripes is mine.</u>

1. looked out the window _____

_____

2. the smallest of the puppies _____

_____

3. the American buffalo _____

_____

4. fell into the pond _____

_____

5. my science class _____

_____

EXERCISE B In the following sentences, underline each subject once and each verb twice. Some sentences may have compound subjects or compound verbs.

EXAMPLES **1.** The <u>pirates</u> <u>dug</u> a hole and <u>buried</u> their treasure.
        2. <u>They</u> <u>had brought</u> the shovel and the box.

1. Before us stood a warrior in armor.

2. Judith lived and worked on a kibbutz in Israel.

3. For the garage sale, Jack and I are collecting old magazines.

4. Jorge and Laura have brought the records.

5. Are you and Lakesha in Girl Scouts?

6. In science class, we studied hurricanes and tracked the storms.

7. Our neighbor feeds corn to his cattle and hogs.

8. My great-grandmother and my great-aunt live in a nursing home.

9. Seth will hike in the wilderness and fish for salmon in Alaska.

10. Will Craig and Ann come to dinner and bring the salad?

Continued ☞

EXERCISE C   On the line provided, write a compound subject for each of the following sentences. When necessary, include proper punctuation.

EXAMPLE 1. At the end of the parade came *the clowns and jugglers.*

1. _____ walked home from the game.

2. _____ chased the rabbit into its hole.

3. In the bright blue package were _____

4. _____ lived in China for many years.

5. Did _____ teach you about horses?

6. _____ have invited me to go to a movie with them.

7. Do _____ have baby-sitting jobs Saturday night?

8. In the reference section of the library were _____

9. _____ were selected to sing in the all-school chorus.

10. Will _____ please come to the information booth?

EXERCISE D   Write a compound verb for each of the following sentences.

EXAMPLE 1. On the first day of spring, we *had a picnic and rode our bikes.*

1. The hockey team _____.

2. On weekends my family _____.

3. After dinner my mother usually _____.

4. Before Thanksgiving we _____.

5. To my surprise the kitten _____.

6. In the summer I _____.

7. At the beginning of every meeting, the scoutmaster _____

_____.

8. At her desk Mikki _____.

9. Despite his fear Bob _____.

10. With a gentle manner the veterinarian _____.

| WORKSHEET 1 | Identifying Direct Objects

EXERCISE A   In each of the following sentences, underline the verb or verb phrase. Then, circle each direct object. If a sentence has no direct object, write *NONE* on the line provided.

EXAMPLES _____ **1.** Could you <u>see</u> our (house) from the plane?

NONE **2.** The film <u>was</u> about life in Argentina.

_____ **1.** Jacques Cousteau co-invented scuba diving equipment.

_____ **2.** Mother measured the length of Sangeeta's new sari.

_____ **3.** An eagle was searching for food.

_____ **4.** Was my poster still in the library?

_____ **5.** I read *National Geographic* every month.

_____ **6.** Lock the door to the shed.

_____ **7.** All campers must bring a swimsuit, sneakers, and a blanket.

_____ **8.** Tell the story to Latoya and him.

_____ **9.** Have you read *The Secret Garden* by Frances Hodgson Burnett?

_____ **10.** My brother and I washed and ironed our clothes.

EXERCISE B   In each of the following sentences, underline the subject once and the verb or verb phrase twice. Then, draw an arrow from the verb to the direct object.

EXAMPLE **1.** That night, the <u>king</u> gladly <u>knighted</u> the squire.

1. The Portuguese established a vast trading empire in the fifteenth century.

2. My brother borrowed my calculator for the week.

3. Did they see the Taj Mahal?

4. Paula prepared the slides for Ms. Stamos.

5. The detective accused the stranger of the crime.

6. I should have kept the combination to my locker.

7. Will you feed my dog over the weekend?

8. Carlos might play the part of the father.

9. Dad is rearranging the furniture again.

10. The thorny branches of the wild rosebushes cut my arms.

LANGUAGE HANDBOOK **8** COMPLEMENTS

| WORKSHEET 2 | **Identifying Direct and Indirect Objects**

EXERCISE A   On the line provided, identify the italicized words in each of the following sentences by writing *DO* for direct objects or *IO* for indirect objects.

EXAMPLE   __DO__   **1.** We all invited our *families* to the class dinner.

_____   **1.** Jovita and Tomás brought *tamales* and *guacamole* for the meal.

_____   **2.** Have you tried *sushi* filled with cream cheese and cucumber?

_____   **3.** Azami gave *Stuart* the recipe for that and other kinds of sushi.

_____   **4.** Semanu, who is from Ghana, served *us* groundnut stew.

_____   **5.** Francesca prepared her family's favorite lasagna *recipe*.

_____   **6.** Jan and Tasha taught *themselves* Thai cooking.

_____   **7.** They served chopped *peanuts* with the spicy, delicious food.

_____   **8.** Josh, Adele, and Buck made the *diners* fresh biscuits, corn bread, and Navajo fry bread.

_____   **9.** Chris and Nehri made Ms. Chen their special cauliflower and potato *curry*.

_____   **10.** Robert and David layered *yogurt* and *raspberries* in a dessert.

EXERCISE B   Identify the direct and indirect objects in each of the following sentences by drawing one line under each direct object and two lines under each indirect object. Some sentences do not have indirect objects.

EXAMPLE **1.** The teacher brought us a book of crossword puzzles.

1. Puzzle makers cleverly challenge me.

2. I give the crossword puzzles serious thought.

3. Reference books offer us information.

4. We ask Mr. Garcia and Ms. Wong questions, too.

5. They always recommend a book to us.

6. Reading books improves my vocabulary and knowledge.

7. For example, Langston Hughes describes the Harlem Renaissance in *The Big Sea*.

8. The cat book showed us a tiger as the largest member of the cat family.

9. Pearl Buck spoke English and Chinese.

10. In addition to being a sculptor, architect, engineer, and scientist, Leonardo da Vinci painted the *Mona Lisa*.

LANGUAGE HANDBOOK **8** COMPLEMENTS

WORKSHEET 3 | **Identifying Direct and Indirect Objects**

EXERCISE A   In the following sentences, underline each indirect object and circle each direct object.

EXAMPLE 1. My mother sold our <u>neighbor</u> my old (toys).

1. Her drum practice is giving us a headache.

2. Marco Polo told people stories about his journey to China.

3. The judge granted the lawyer a recess.

4. Mom taught my brother chess.

5. The manager sent her customers cards.

6. Juana loaned him her car.

7. Julian read Dad a poem by Joseph Bruchac.

8. The experiment showed the class the danger of fire.

9. Uncle Vincente packed me a lunch for the bus trip.

10. The old trader sold us a piece of feldspar.

EXERCISE B   For each sentence, fill in the appropriate blanks with the direct and indirect objects. If there is no object, write *NONE* in the blank or blanks.

EXAMPLES 1. Mrs. Bell showed Beth her experiment.

Direct object: ____*experiment*____   Indirect object: _____*Beth*_____

2. Heather ran to the top of the stairs.

Direct object: ____*NONE*____   Indirect object: ____*NONE*____

1. The answers are in the back of the book.

Direct object: _____   Indirect object: _____

2. Jakob and Wilhelm Grimm collected German folk tales.

Direct object: _____   Indirect object: _____

3. Will you make us a salad for lunch?

Direct object: _____   Indirect object: _____

4. Students on the committee will report to the auditorium.

Direct object: _____   Indirect object: _____

5. We visit old friends during the holidays.

Direct object: _____   Indirect object: _____

LANGUAGE
HANDBOOK **8** COMPLEMENTS

| WORKSHEET 4 | **Identifying Subject Complements** |

EXERCISE A   Underline the linking verb in each of the following sentences. Then, circle the subject complement.

EXAMPLE **1.** Our Chihuahua is a good (watchdog).

1. Seoul is the capital of South Korea.

2. A peach would taste good right now.

3. Reggie became an engineer after college.

4. Thai Garden is a restaurant that serves good spring rolls.

5. With practice, you can be a good musician.

6. Does a green hat look good with a purple shirt?

7. These plums seem ripe to me.

8. Some Indians are Muslims.

9. Remain calm during the award ceremony.

10. Bianca's voice sounded sad.

EXERCISE B   Each of the following sentences contains a subject complement in italics. On the line provided, identify the complement as *N* for noun, *PRON* for pronoun, or *ADJ* for adjective. Draw a line under each verb or verb phrase.

EXAMPLES ___N___ **1.** He will be the *judge* at the fair.

PRON **2.** The woman in the blue dress, our leader, is *she*.

ADJ **3.** The sky was *blue* and sunny.

_____ **1.** Mr. Shapiro seemed *cheerful* about the change of plan.

_____ **2.** Is she your *sister*?

_____ **3.** The Mexican artist Diego Rivera was *famous* for his murals.

_____ **4.** Lee's partner in the doubles tennis match was *she*.

_____ **5.** Are you *happy* with your new math teacher?

_____ **6.** They remained good *friends* for many years.

_____ **7.** Those lemons were too *sour*.

_____ **8.** Next time, the winners will be *they*.

_____ **9.** The capital of Louisiana is *Baton Rouge*.

_____ **10.** Paolo became *interested* in Italian art.

| WORKSHEET 5 | Identifying and Using the Predicate Nominative

EXERCISE A   Some of the following sentences contain a predicate nominative. Others do not. If a sentence has a predicate nominative, write the predicate nominative on the line provided. If a sentence does not contain a predicate nominative, write *NONE*.

EXAMPLES   _____birthday_____   **1.** Monday is my dad's birthday.

_____NONE_____   **2.** He is leaving for Bolivia tomorrow.

_____ **1.** The Dutch founded Cape Town in South Africa.

_____ **2.** Mr. Tan became skipper of the boat.

_____ **3.** The boat was made of wood and had sails.

_____ **4.** I am a member of the basketball team.

_____ **5.** Gymnastics is the first event on the schedule.

_____ **6.** My father has been a bricklayer for ten years.

_____ **7.** Orchids can be grown in a greenhouse.

_____ **8.** A good pet is also a good friend.

_____ **9.** Julius Lester became active in the civil rights movement.

_____ **10.** Knowledge is the gift of time.

EXERCISE B   Write a suitable predicate nominative on the line provided. Do not use the same predicate nominative twice.

EXAMPLE   **1.** Abraham Lincoln was *a fine public speaker.*

1. My favorite sport remains _____.

2. After graduation, I will become a _____.

3. The most important thing for a picnic is _____.

4. The person who brought flowers was _____.

5. Two of my favorite stories are _____.

6. My grandmother's favorite holiday was _____.

7. Until today, the leader had been _____.

8. Your reading assignment for tomorrow will be _____.

9. Our solar system is _____.

10. Hawaii became _____.

LANGUAGE HANDBOOK **8** COMPLEMENTS

| WORKSHEET 6 | Identifying and Using Predicate Adjectives

EXERCISE A   Underline each predicate adjective in the following sentences.

EXAMPLES   **1.** Are your sentences <u>clear</u> and <u>complete</u>?

2. The onions and garlic smelled <u>delicious</u>.

1. Will these flowers stay fresh for a week?

2. Langston Hughes was often lonesome as a boy.

3. Puppies are usually eager for a romp.

4. Wheat grew tall in the fields.

5. Emily Dickinson's poems are usually short.

6. His behavior at dinner was perfect.

7. Must a library always be so quiet?

8. Our new truck will be blue and white.

9. You must be sharp and alert for this test.

10. Could you become rich and famous?

EXERCISE B   For each of the following sentences, write at least one appropriate predicate adjective on the lines provided.

EXAMPLE   **1.** A hiker should be *alert and agile.* _____

1. Suddenly, the sky grew _____.

2. My friends were soaked by the storm, but I stayed _____.

3. Our cat is _____.

4. The lunches at our school are _____.

5. You certainly sound _____ about your prize.

6. Does your grandmother seem _____ with her birthday present?

7. Professor Mahmoud was _____ about the results of her experiment.

8. He felt _____ after taking the cold medicine.

9. My dog Rocky is both _____ and _____.

10. She remained _____ even though the other players were worried.

LANGUAGE
HANDBOOK **8** COMPLEMENTS

WORKSHEET 7 | **Identifying Predicate Nominatives and Predicate Adjectives**

EXERCISE . Underline the subject complement in each of the following sentences. On the line provided, write *PN* if it is a predicate nominative or *PA* if it is a predicate adjective.

EXAMPLES ____*PN*____ 1. Our new puppy is a <u>German shepherd</u>.

____*PA*____ 2. I was too <u>early</u> for my appointment.

_____ 1. The test on the French Revolution was not difficult.

_____ 2. Velázquez was a Spanish artist.

_____ 3. Of the Greek goddesses, Aphrodite was the most beautiful.

_____ 4. Jody will become the new captain of the soccer team.

_____ 5. Sloths are very slow animals.

_____ 6. The taco sauce tasted too hot for me.

_____ 7. This path is a shortcut to the parking lot.

_____ 8. Trevor and his brother have always remained good at painting.

_____ 9. Your granola mix is delicious!

_____ 10. Asha might become the club's official secretary.

_____ 11. The sky appears hazy today.

_____ 12. The elephants will be the leaders of the circus parade.

_____ 13. Mr. Garcia became assistant principal last week.

_____ 14. Many baby clothes are soft.

_____ 15. Doesn't the fresh herb bread smell wonderful?

_____ 16. A sheik is an Arab leader.

_____ 17. When Harriet Tubman and other escaped slaves traveled, they had to remain silent.

_____ 18. Every noise could sound loud and cause them to be recaptured.

_____ 19. Our team can be the quiz bowl champions if we continue to do well.

_____ 20. The beans I planted for the science fair grew very tall.

_____ 21. My cousin Bridget became a captain in the Army Reserves.

_____ 22. The mattress is too firm.

_____ 23. This recipe for corn bread looks easy.

_____ 24. *North by Northwest* is my father's favorite movie.

_____ 25. Is this fruit fresh?

LANGUAGE HANDBOOK 8 COMPLEMENTS

WORKSHEET 8 Test

EXERCISE A   Underline the verb in each of the following sentences. Circle each complement. On the line provided, write *AV* if the verb is used as an action verb. Write *LV* if the verb is used as a linking verb.

EXAMPLE _____AV_____ 1. Do you smell a (fire)?

_____ 1. Canadian biologist Kit Kovacs studies seals.

_____ 2. Bring me today's newspaper.

_____ 3. The casserole in the oven smells good!

_____ 4. My mother is a doctor of medicine.

_____ 5. Can a mongoose kill a cobra?

_____ 6. In time, the caterpillar becomes a butterfly.

_____ 7. Yolanda locked the door on her way out.

_____ 8. Dan's idea for our African American history project is good.

_____ 9. The experience taught me the value of money.

_____ 10. Have you tasted the peaches?

EXERCISE B   Underline each direct object and each indirect object in the following sentences. Then, over each direct object, write *DO*. Over each indirect object, write *IO*. If a sentence does not contain an indirect object or a direct object, write *NONE* on the line provided.

EXAMPLES _____ 1. Todd loaned his cousin and her an old comedy film.
  IO .... *IO* .... *DO*

_____NONE_____ 2. The children colored carefully inside the lines.

_____ 1. The gloves fit me perfectly!

_____ 2. Grandma gave Tamara a recipe for couscous.

_____ 3. We need two more forks, one napkin, and a knife.

_____ 4. The wax museum had statues of many famous people.

_____ 5. Besnik showed Pilar and Hal the baby chickens.

_____ 6. Take your brother and his friend some more blankets.

_____ 7. They jumped quickly into the pool of cool water.

_____ 8. Mrs. Stamos teaches adults basic English.

_____ 9. Will you write her and him a letter from Mississippi?

_____ 10. The peoples of New Guinea speak many languages.

Continued ☞

EXERCISE C   Underline each subject complement in the following sentences. Above each predicate nominative, write *PN*. Over each predicate adjective, write *PA*. If a sentence has no complement, write *NONE* on the line provided.

EXAMPLES   _____   **1.** After three hours of football practice, I was <u>weary</u> and <u>sore</u>.
                                                                                                                              PA   PA

   ___NONE___   **2.** The child nodded solemnly in agreement.

_____   **1.** Kilauea is a volcano in Hawaii.

_____   **2.** My hometown is San Francisco.

_____   **3.** I am very sorry for your trouble.

_____   **4.** The paintings of Salvador Dali remain popular.

_____   **5.** The clerks at the grocery store are courteous and helpful.

_____   **6.** Rome was once the cultural center of the Western world.

_____   **7.** The judge's decision will be final.

_____   **8.** The planets between Earth and the Sun are Mercury and Venus.

_____   **9.** Will Mayor Robinson speak at the banquet?

_____   **10.** That Shetland pony seems gentle, but it can be frisky.

EXERCISE D   Underline the complements in the following sentences. On the line provided, identify the complement as *DO* for direct object, *IO* for indirect object, *PN* for predicate nominative, or *PA* for predicate adjective.

EXAMPLES   ___PA___   **1.** That collie of yours seems <u>friendly</u> to me.

   ___IO, DO___   **2.** Did you give <u>Mrs. Grant</u> your <u>name</u>?

_____   **1.** Have you read the biography of Harriet Tubman?

_____   **2.** Stacy has become a very good runner.

_____   **3.** All the food at the party was Swedish.

_____   **4.** Our next stop will be Buenos Aires.

_____   **5.** Inca society was highly structured.

_____   **6.** My sister has read *Black Beauty* several times.

_____   **7.** Those photographs are not bad at all.

_____   **8.** Will you lend me your atlas?

_____   **9.** That bright star in the sky is really a planet.

_____   **10.** I sold Jamie the old sled in the garage.

LANGUAGE HANDBOOK 9 — KINDS OF SENTENCES

| WORKSHEET 1 | Identifying Simple and Compound Sentences |

EXERCISE In the following sentences, underline each subject once and each verb twice. Circle *C* if the sentence is compound and *S* if the sentence is simple. Remember that a simple sentence may have compound parts.

Ⓒ S   **EXAMPLE 1.** I <u>used</u> paints for my picture, but <u>she</u> and <u>Sam</u> <u>used</u> pencils.

C   S   **1.** Many Hopi, Apache, and Navajo live in Arizona.

C   S   **2.** Navajo silversmiths make beautiful jewelry, and Navajo weavers create stunning rugs.

C   S   **3.** Would you most like to travel in Europe, South America, Africa, or Asia?

C   S   **4.** There are so many interesting places to go in the world!

C   S   **5.** Our dog brought the newspaper in; however, it was the neighbor's paper.

C   S   **6.** Our class earns money to give to the local humane society, and some of us also help care for the animals at the animal shelter.

C   S   **7.** Milly can't have a pet at home, but she plays with animals at the shelter.

C   S   **8.** She and Tyrel go to the shelter on Wednesdays and help clean the cages.

C   S   **9.** The shelter manager has prepared a flyer about how to be a responsible pet owner, and we hand out the flyers to people.

C   S   **10.** All pets appreciate love and good care.

C   S   **11.** Javier or Denise usually bowls on Saturday morning.

C   S   **12.** Of all the horses in the stable, Lucky and Red run the fastest.

C   S   **13.** Our runner tripped over a hurdle, yet she finished first.

C   S   **14.** Members of the Ecology Club chose a highway and picked up litter.

C   S   **15.** We entered by the side door, and we left the same way.

C   S   **16.** Argentina and Venezuela are in South America.

C   S   **17.** They found no silver in the old mine.

C   S   **18.** Golf requires a steady hand, and rugby requires a good deal of energy.

C   S   **19.** We went to the car show, but Dad stayed home.

C   S   **20.** Otis kicked the ball past the goalie and scored the winning point.

C   S   **21.** Twenty-seven students are in Tiffany's class, and thirty students are in Eric's class

C   S   **22.** My brother just fixed the flat tire and put the tire back on his bicycle.

C   S   **23.** The cat and dog played or slept during the day.

C   S   **24.** Aaron mowed the lawn, and Holly trimmed the bushes.

C   S   **25.** Three brass bands, twelve horses, and six floats were in the parade.

LANGUAGE
HANDBOOK **9** KINDS OF SENTENCES

| WORKSHEET 2 | Using Simple and Compound Sentences

EXERCISE On the lines provided, rewrite the following sentences as indicated in parentheses after each sentence.

EXAMPLES 1. Jalisco is a state in western Mexico. Guadalajara is the capital of Jalisco. (*compound sentence*) _Jalisco is a state in western Mexico, and its capital is Guadalajara._

2. The armadillo, an unusual mammal, is found from Missouri to South America, and it is known for its bony plates of armor. (*two simple sentences*) _The armadillo, an unusual mammal, is found from Missouri to South America. It is known for its bony plates of armor._

1. The word *Mexico* comes from a Nahuatl word for a god of war, and the word is used as the name of the country, a state in the country, and a gulf. (*two simple sentences*)

_____

_____

_____

2. Thurgood Marshall was born in 1908, and he became an associate justice of the United States Supreme Court in 1967. (*two simple sentences*) _____

_____

_____

_____

3. Jaguars are wild cats. Ocelots are wild cats. Both may be found in North and South America. (*compound sentence*) _____

_____

_____

_____

4. Alberta and British Columbia are provinces of western Canada, and Nova Scotia and Prince Edward Island are provinces of eastern Canada. (*two simple sentences*)_____

_____

_____

_____

Continued ☞

5. The Art Club is going to the exhibit of Inca art on Tuesday. I have to go to a Spanish Club meeting that night. *(compound sentence)* _____

_____

_____

_____

6. The houses on our block now are all painted white, but several of the neighbors are talking about repainting with dark colors. *(two simple sentences)* _____

_____

_____

_____

7. My favorite subject is math. My cousin's favorite subject is English. *(compound sentence)* _____

_____

_____

_____

8. Our soccer team is number one in the district, and according to our coach, our baseball team will place well in district competitions. *(two simple sentences)* _____

_____

_____

_____

9. Some people like pens that make a thick line. I prefer a pen that makes a very thin line. *(compound sentence)* _____

_____

_____

_____

10. Sandra and Enrico want to be on the student council. They plan to register and start campaigning next week. *(compound sentence)* _____

_____

_____

_____

LANGUAGE HANDBOOK 9 KINDS OF SENTENCES

| WORKSHEET 3 | **Classifying Sentences by Purpose** |

EXERCISE Add an appropriate end mark to each sentence. Then, on the line provided, label the sentence as *DEC* for declarative, *IMP* for imperative, *INT* for interrogative, or *EXC* for exclamatory.

EXAMPLES   __DEC__ **1.** Reindeer cautiously stepped on the frozen lake.

   __INT__ **2.** Will soccer practice be over by 7:00 P.M.?

_____ **1.** Keep out

_____ **2.** Jay and Lou practice guitar in our garage

_____ **3.** Hieroglyphs are one of the earliest forms of writing

_____ **4.** We tried that magic trick, but it did not work

_____ **5.** Are you a member of the Spanish Club

_____ **6.** What a beautiful horse that is

_____ **7.** Take your time

_____ **8.** *Côte d'Ivoire* is French for Ivory Coast

_____ **9.** Is she your best friend

_____ **10.** Imagine how we laughed

_____ **11.** His maps of ancient Greece hung on every wall in the house

_____ **12.** Did you solve the problem

_____ **13.** Be careful with that expensive vase

_____ **14.** Obey the rules of the road

_____ **15.** How happy we were

_____ **16.** We played table tennis in the basement

_____ **17.** Take that basketball outside immediately

_____ **18.** The bus goes to Tikal, Guatemala

_____ **19.** What is the state flower of Montana

_____ **20.** Get the baby away from the stove

_____ **21.** We went to see a movie yesterday

_____ **22.** Did you see that new science fiction film

_____ **23.** What a terrific movie

_____ **24.** Buy the tickets early

_____ **25.** Dean and Frank got off the plane

WORKSHEET 4 | **Classifying Sentences by Purpose**

EXERCISE A   On the line provided, identify each of the following sentences as *DEC* for declarative, *INT* for interrogative, *IMP* for imperative, or *EXC* for exclamatory.

EXAMPLES __*EXC*__ **1.** How interesting this story is!

__*INT*__ **2.** Why is this story interesting?

_____ **1.** Have you read Virginia Driving Hawk Sneve's story "The Medicine Bag"?

_____ **2.** Sneve writes books about American Indian life.

_____ **3.** Return those books to the library when you finish.

_____ **4.** The smiley faces on that deck of cards are so funny.

_____ **5.** Where shall we sit when we go to the game?

_____ **6.** Stay alert when you ride a bike.

_____ **7.** Watch out for that loose gravel.

_____ **8.** Have you ever seen a lacrosse game?

_____ **9.** The game was first played by North American Indians.

_____ **10.** Wow, it can be an exciting game!

EXERCISE B   On the lines provided, write sentences according to the directions given. End each sentence with the proper punctuation.

EXAMPLES **1.** Write a sentence that states a fact.

Earth is the third planet from the Sun.

2. Write a sentence that expresses surprise.

I didn't know that!

1. Write a sentence that is a polite request.

_____

_____

_____

2. Write a sentence that expresses excitement.

_____

_____

_____

Continued ☞

3. Write a sentence that is a command.

_____

_____

_____

4. Write a sentence that requests directions.

_____

_____

_____

5. Write a sentence that gives information.

_____

_____

_____

6. Write a sentence that expresses fear.

_____

_____

_____

7. Write a sentence that is a strong command.

_____

_____

_____

8. Write a sentence that makes a statement.

_____

_____

_____

9. Write a sentence that asks about something.

_____

_____

_____

10. Write a sentence that shows excitement.

_____

_____

_____

LANGUAGE HANDBOOK **9** **KINDS OF SENTENCES**

| WORKSHEET 5 | Test |

EXERCISE A Read the sentences below. If a sentence is simple, write *S* on the line provided. If a sentence is compound, write *C*.

EXAMPLE ___C___ **1.** Yolanda has a parakeet, and Carl owns a hamster.

_____ **1.** I must hurry, or I will be late for school.

_____ **2.** Tanya loves lettuce but will not eat cabbage.

_____ **3.** Leif Ericson sailed from Greenland and landed in North America around A.D. 1000.

_____ **4.** The clouds were dark, but the sun still shone.

_____ **5.** We cleared the table, and Rosa and Javier did the dishes.

_____ **6.** Jason and Julia invited us for dinner and served us beans and rice.

_____ **7.** He turned on the radio, but he did not pay any attention to the announcer or the music.

_____ **8.** Sarah finished the book and put it back on the shelf.

_____ **9.** Lewis Carroll wrote *Alice in Wonderland*, and Sir John Tenniel created the illustrations.

_____ **10.** Shel Silverstein wrote and illustrated *Where the Sidewalk Ends*.

EXERCISE B Add an appropriate punctuation mark to the end of each sentence. On the line provided, identify each sentence as *DEC* for declarative, *IMP* for imperative, *INT* for interrogative, or *EXC* for exclamatory.

EXAMPLE ___EXC___ **1.** How we laughed at that monkey's tricks*!*

_____ **1.** How are you feeling

_____ **2.** Stop that noise immediately

_____ **3.** The Anasazi were cliff-dwelling American Indians

_____ **4.** How sunny the kitchen is

_____ **5.** Take these papers home for your parents' signatures

_____ **6.** I found the recipe in an old cookbook

_____ **7.** What a beautiful day this is

_____ **8.** What do you think of this book

_____ **9.** Bring me a pencil

_____ **10.** Where did you put my coat

Continued ☞

EXERCISE C   Add words to each of the following sentences to make it a compound sentence. When you are finished, you should have ten compound sentences.

EXAMPLES 1. My baby brother must have his own way, or *he begins to cry.*

2. The dogs started to bark, and *the raccoon ran up the tree.*

1. Maricela mowed the lawn today, but _____

_____

2. Captain Janeway gave the order, and _____

_____

3. You must practice every day, or _____

_____

4. Our television set is old, yet _____

_____

5. My sister goes to Huston-Tillotson College, and _____

_____

6. In class, I read the poem "Oranges" by Gary Soto, so _____

_____

7. I cooked dinner, and _____

_____

8. The whistle blew, for _____

_____

9. Our dog is very small, but _____

_____

10. You must arrive on time, or _____

_____

10 WRITING EFFECTIVE SENTENCES

| WORSHEET 1 | **Identifying Complete Sentences and Sentence Fragments** |

EXERCISE Some of the following word groups are sentences, and some are not. On the line provided, write *CS* if a word group is a complete sentence. Write *SF* if a word group is a sentence fragment.

EXAMPLES   _*SF*_   1. Bought the last purple sneakers in the store.

           _*CS*_   2. I wore them home.

_____ **1.** Sisal, a strong fiber used to make rope and twine in Kenya.

_____ **2.** Quickly, the cat ran under the car and escaped the dog.

_____ **3.** A white boat with a green sunshade over the back of it.

_____ **4.** Too many reasons for too many things.

_____ **5.** Never play your trumpet during dinner.

_____ **6.** A large vocabulary is, of course, an advantage to anyone.

_____ **7.** Are these chocolates from Switzerland?

_____ **8.** Her magnificent marble sculpture of a family.

_____ **9.** By three o'clock in the afternoon next Friday.

_____ **10.** Few people can draw pictures as good as these.

_____ **11.** Decided on a compromise between the two groups of students.

_____ **12.** Birago Diop is one of Africa's best-known writers.

_____ **13.** Calling for a recount of the votes.

_____ **14.** Under the soft feather pillow at the head of the bed.

_____ **15.** Today nearly all Turks are Muslims.

_____ **16.** The first clear day in the spring of that year.

_____ **17.** A pair of robins is making a nest in our oak tree.

_____ **18.** Questioning everyone in the room.

_____ **19.** Iceland is a large island in the North Atlantic.

_____ **20.** At the very top of the stairs stood a woman in an evening dress.

_____ **21.** Speaking on the phone to a friend in Germany.

_____ **22.** Watch out for potholes when you are riding your bicycle.

_____ **23.** Before she left for Santa Fe.

_____ **24.** My favorite writer, Chinua Achebe.

_____ **25.** Did anyone see last night's episode of *Seventh Heaven*?

LANGUAGE HANDBOOK **10** WRITING EFFECTIVE SENTENCES

| WORKSHEET 2 | Identifying and Correcting Sentence Fragments

EXERCISE A On each line provided, write *CS* if the word group is a complete sentence. If the word group is a sentence fragment, write *SF*.

EXAMPLES ___*CS*___ 1. We are cooking dinner tonight since Mom must work late.

___*SF*___ 2. Since we got our new kitten.

_____ 1. When the pitcher throws the ball.

_____ 2. The indigenous, or native, people of the Caribbean islands.

_____ 3. If it doesn't rain, we'll have our picnic on Sunday.

_____ 4. Because the bus was late, Mr. Davis drove us to school.

_____ 5. Unless you include a full address on every envelope.

_____ 6. Call me when dinner is ready.

_____ 7. North America one of the most culturally diverse regions in the world.

_____ 8. Dreaming about our vacation in the mountains.

_____ 9. Will you meet me out front after the movie is over?

_____ 10. Please be quiet when I'm talking on the phone!

EXERCISE B Each numbered item contains two word groups. If one of the word groups is a fragment, connect the fragment to the other word group and write the complete sentence on the lines provided. If both word groups are already complete sentences, write *CS* on the line provided.

EXAMPLE 1. Because they hunt at night. Owls are rarely seen during the day.
Because they hunt at night, owls are rarely seen during the day.

1. While snow fell softly on the roof. We slept soundly in our beds. _____

_____

2. Although the day was cloudy, I still got a sunburn. I was sore for three days. _____

_____

3. The bridge was up. A tall ship was coming through. _____

_____

4. We stood in line with everyone else. Waiting to get into the theater. _____

_____

5. Guatemalan farmers grow corn, beans, and squash. Like their Maya ancestors. _____

_____

LANGUAGE
HANDBOOK **10 WRITING EFFECTIVE SENTENCES**

| WORKSHEET 3 | **Correcting Sentence Fragments**

EXERCISE A   On the lines provided, either add words to make the fragment a complete sentence or connect the fragment with a sentence. Be sure to use correct capitalization and punctuation.

> **EXAMPLES 1.** Although light appears colorless. It is actually made up of many colors.
> *Although light appears colorless, it is actually made up of many colors.*
>
> **2.** On my birthday. *On my birthday, I'd like to see a movie.*

1. On every afternoon but Sunday. _____

_____

2. After I learn Morse code. We can send messages. _____

_____

3. When the rain stopped. _____

_____

4. Do not leave the house. While I am gone. _____

_____

5. Underneath the biggest tree on the hill. _____

_____

6. An excellent kite maker. My cousin also makes model trains. _____

_____

7. Since the discoveries of Gregor Mendel. Farmers have been able to breed superior plants.

_____

_____

8. Beech trees are called deciduous. Because they shed leaves every year. _____

_____

_____

9. If you have the time. Look at *The Gleaners*. A painting by Jean François Millet. _____

_____

_____

10. Amelia checked the dictionary. While Tranh checked the encyclopedia. _____

_____

_____

Continued ☞

LANGUAGE HANDBOOK 10 WORSHEET 3 *(continued)*

EXERCISE B   Correct each of the five sentence fragments in the following paragraph by rewriting the sentences on the lines provided. Be sure to use correct capitalization and punctuation.

> **EXAMPLE**   When we first moved to Florida. I made an amazing discovery at the beach.
>
> *When we first moved to Florida, I made an amazing discovery at the beach.*

While I was digging in the sand. I discovered some strange shells. When I asked my grandmother about them. She recognized them right away. They were coquinas. Small, brightly colored shells. Amazingly, of the hundreds of them. No two were alike. They were pink, blue, and lavender. Some were striped, and some were not. While they stayed alive in the salt water and under the sand, they remained beautiful. However, when I took them out of the salt water. They lost their beauty.

_____

_____

_____

_____

_____

_____

_____

_____

_____

_____

_____

_____

_____

_____

_____

_____

_____

_____

_____

_____

_____

_____

LANGUAGE HANDBOOK 10 WRITING EFFECTIVE SENTENCES

| WORKSHEET 4 | Identifying and Correcting Run-on Sentences

EXERCISE A On the line provided, write *CS* for each correct sentence and *R* for each run-on sentence.

EXAMPLES ___CS___ 1. Above us soared an eagle, one of the last of its kind.

___R___ 2. Many eagles are endangered species they are protected by law.

_____ 1. Unless we can borrow some extra chairs, some people will have to stand.

_____ 2. I've been to Texas, but I have never crossed the Rio Grande.

_____ 3. We need one more person for the game, will you play?

_____ 4. Be very careful with those glasses your grandmother brought them all the way from Germany.

_____ 5. Without a doubt, the *Mona Lisa* is the world's most famous portrait.

_____ 6. Tomorrow is our last day in Washington, D.C., let's visit the Smithsonian.

_____ 7. Fragrant gardenias were heaped in a pile on the table their beauty was reflected by a mirror underneath them.

_____ 8. It was the last inning of the game, the bases were loaded.

_____ 9. We hurried home to watch Mom on the news.

_____ 10. Miranda entered the first opening in the maze she was lost.

EXERCISE B On the lines provided, separate each run-on sentence into two sentences. Punctuate and capitalize each sentence correctly. If a sentence is already correct, write *C*.

EXAMPLES 1. What do you have for lunch, I have a sandwich and an apple. *What do you have for lunch? I have a sandwich and an apple.*

2. Maybe they didn't know better, but you did. *C*

1. These batteries are great, they've been working for months. _____

_____

_____

2. Although she has been here only one year, Han speaks English perfectly. _____

_____

_____

Continued ☞

LANGUAGE HANDBOOK **10** **WORKSHEET 4** (continued)

3. Take your time there's no need for a big rush. _____

_____

_____

4. Kareem is probably over at Nina's, they are working on Nina's bike. _____

_____

_____

5. What a beautiful day this is may we go on a picnic? _____

_____

_____

EXERCISE C   Decide where the sentences in the following paragraph begin and end. Insert capital letters and end marks. Draw a line through lowercase letters that should be capitalized.

　　　　　　　　　　　　　　　　　　　　　　　　　　　　　D
EXAMPLE My old computer is too slow. do you think I need a new one**?**

　　My brand-new computer had just arrived in the mail eagerly, I opened the boxes the

computer inside was wrapped in plastic and was held securely in place by foam on top of

the computer was a small instruction book I put the book aside, tore open the plastic, and

carefully lifted the computer out of the box then, I took it over to the table next, I went

back to the box and found a plastic bag full of cords it was time for a look at the

instructions where had I put the manual a half-hour later, I found it under the empty

boxes

LANGUAGE HANDBOOK **10** WRITING EFFECTIVE SENTENCES

| WORKSHEET 5 | **Revising Stringy Sentences**

EXERCISE Most of the following sentences are stringy. On the lines provided, revise each stringy sentence by breaking it into two or more sentences. If none of the sentences in an item need improving, write *C*.

EXAMPLE **1.** Snapping turtles eat small water animals, and they also feed on plants and algae, and snappers have strong jaws, and they can bite hard. _Snapping turtles eat small water_ _animals. They also feed on plants and algae. Snappers have_ _strong jaws, and they can bite hard._

1. In 1912, Garrett Morgan created a gas mask, and this device had a canvas hood, and the hood was connected to a special breathing tube. _____

_____

_____

2. Bonnie spent a week at summer camp. There she learned canoeing and swimming and made several new friends. When the week was over, Bonnie did not want to leave. _____

_____

_____

_____

3. The creek had flooded, and no cars could cross the bridge, and there was no way for us to get home. _____

_____

_____

_____

4. Kathy loosened the soil with a hoe, and Miguel planted the tomato plants two feet apart, and finally they watered the new garden and took a break. _____

_____

_____

_____

Continued ☞

5. My brother helped me study my lines, and soon I knew most of them by heart, and I enjoyed being in the play, and I would like to be in another one next year. _____

_____

_____

_____

6. The sun was bright, and the breeze was gentle and cool, and the children played happily all morning. _____

_____

_____

_____

7. The runners lined up in the starting blocks, and the starter's pistol was fired, and Carl Lewis quickly took the lead. _____

_____

_____

_____

8. Of the main Japanese islands, Shikoku is the smallest. It covers about 7,000 square miles. _____

_____

_____

_____

9. We chose a shaded, level spot near the river, and Mom set up the tent, and Lani and I unloaded the rest of the gear. _____

_____

_____

_____

10. Phil Roman studied at the Los Angeles Art Center, and he got his first animation job in 1955, and Roman eventually went on to become the president of his own animation studio. _____

_____

_____

_____

LANGUAGE HANDBOOK 10 WRITING EFFECTIVE SENTENCES

WORKSHEET 6 | **Using Adjectives and Adverbs to Combine Sentences**

EXERCISE Combine each of the following groups of sentences by taking words from one sentence and adding them to another sentence. Write one complete sentence on the line provided.

EXAMPLE **1.** The French castle had a door. The castle was ancient. *The ancient French castle had a door.*

1. No one had discovered the door. The door was secret. _____

_____

2. At last, it was found. It was found accidentally. _____

_____

3. A woman was cleaning a bookcase. The bookcase was dusty. _____

_____

4. She found a lever. The lever was very small. It was wooden. _____

_____

5. She turned the doorknob. She turned it carefully. _____

_____

6. A door opened. The door was big. It opened suddenly. _____

_____

7. She told everyone about it. She told them excitedly. _____

_____

8. Beyond the door was a hallway. The hallway was dark. The hallway was mysterious.

_____

_____

9. The woman lit a candle. The candle was small. She lit it quickly. _____

_____

_____

10. Inside, she found a room with a chair and a photograph of a woman. The room was small. The photograph was old. The woman in the photograph was young and beautiful. _____

_____

_____

LANGUAGE
HANDBOOK **10** **WRITING EFFECTIVE SENTENCES**

| WORKSHEET 7 | **Using Adjective Phrases and Adverb Phrases to Combine Sentences** |

EXERCISE   On the lines provided, combine each group of sentences into one sentence by taking a prepositional phrase from one sentence and adding it to another sentence.

> **EXAMPLE 1.** A family lives in the woods. It is a family of rabbits. The woods are near our house. _A family of rabbits lives in the woods near our house._

1. Would you get the groceries? Get them from the car. _____
_____

2. Light snow fell. The snow fell on our heads. _____
_____

3. The sun was setting. It was setting behind the trees. _____
_____

4. We saw a sculpture. The sculpture was by Picasso. _____
_____

5. A skillful captain guided the boat. He guided it through the dangerous channel. _____
_____
_____

6. Underline the misspelled words. The words are in the next paragraph. _____
_____
_____

7. Cardamom is a popular spice. It is in many foods of South Asia. _____
_____
_____

8. A tiny brook trickled. It trickled down the mountain. The mountain was near our cabin. _____
_____

9. The bell rang. The bell was in the tower. The bell rang at noon. _____
_____
_____

10. A friend lost his coat. He is a friend of my brother's. He lost his coat on the bus. _____
_____
_____

LANGUAGE
HANDBOOK **10 WRITING EFFECTIVE SENTENCES**

WORKSHEET 8 | Using Compound Subjects and Compound Verbs to Combine Sentences

EXERCISE On the lines provided, use either a compound subject or a compound verb to combine the sentences in each item into one complete sentence.

EXAMPLE 1. Dad lit the kerosene lamp. He hung it in our tent. _Dad lit the kerosene lamp and hung it in our tent._

1. The detectives investigated the case. They found no solution. _____
   _____

2. A bulldozer dug the hole for the building. It piled dirt into a hill. _____
   _____

3. Did you study for the Spanish test last night? Did you watch television last night? ____
   _____

4. We went to the beach. We had a picnic. We did not swim. _____
   _____

5. Mrs. Strauss is showing a film today. So is Mr. Batista. _____
   _____

6. German is spoken in Switzerland. French is also spoken there. _____
   _____

7. A blue scarf would go well with that jacket. A red scarf would go well, too. _____
   _____

8. The best drawings will go to the state fair. The best sculptures will go to the state fair.
   _____

9. Will you give your speech first? Will Dalton give his speech first? Will Kim give her speech first? _____
   _____
   _____

10. I like turnips. I don't enjoy carrots. _____
    _____
    _____

LANGUAGE
HANDBOOK **10** WRITING EFFECTIVE SENTENCES

| WORKSHEET 9 | Using Conjunctions and Connecting Words to Combine Sentences

EXERCISE A   On the line provided, write a conjunction or connecting word that could combine the two sentences into one compound sentence.

EXAMPLE ____*or*____ 1. I may go to Spain this year. I may go to France instead.

_____ 1. Fish were jumping. Birds were singing on this beautiful day.

_____ 2. Mom might say yes. She might say no.

_____ 3. Belgium is a country in northwestern Europe. It is known for its fine lace.

_____ 4. The key fits the lock. The key won't turn.

_____ 5. Kittens were playing in the kitchen. They had found a bag on the floor.

_____ 6. I waved to my friends from the helicopter. They looked up.

_____ 7. It's a costume party to celebrate Mardi Gras. Let's decide what to wear.

_____ 8. The computer's disk drive could be the problem. The disk could be faulty.

_____ 9. The violin sounds fine. The piano is not in tune.

_____ 10. Rainbows result from moisture in the air. The sun shines on the drops of rain.

EXERCISE B   On the lines provided, use a conjunction to combine each of the following groups of sentences into one compound sentence.

EXAMPLE 1. You may go to the library. You can check out only three books. *You may go to the library, but you can check out only three books.*

1. Hurry up. You'll be late. _____

_____

_____

_____

2. The sun was shining. Rain was pouring down. _____

_____

_____

_____

Continued ☞

3. We planted the Dutch tulip bulbs by the sidewalk. They bloomed early in the spring.

_____

_____

_____

4. Uncle Chen likes his new boots. The boots are too tight. _____

_____

_____

5. You may order vegetable soup. You may order a sandwich. _____

_____

_____

_____

6. The band was playing. No one was dancing. _____

_____

_____

_____

7. Latoya oiled the sewing machine. It works much better now. _____

_____

_____

_____

8. The name *Iceland* sounds cold. Iceland's coastal temperatures are mild. _____

_____

_____

_____

9. The sailboat signaled the bridge keeper. He raised the bridge. _____

_____

_____

_____

10. You must arrive at eight o'clock. We will leave without you. _____

_____

_____

_____

LANGUAGE HANDBOOK 10 WRITING EFFECTIVE SENTENCES

| WORKSHEET 10 | Using Connecting Words to Combine Sentences

EXERCISE A   Combine each pair of sentences by writing one complete sentence using a connecting word such as *after, because, since, when, whether,* or *while.*

EXAMPLE **1.** I was sewing the hem. My sister was sewing on buttons.
    While I was sewing the hem, my sister was sewing on buttons.

1. You should set a good example for your brothers. They look up to you. _____
_____
_____

2. The final votes were counted. Sandra was the new student president. _____
_____
_____

3. I don't know. It will rain today or tomorrow. _____
_____
_____

4. Mari moved here last year from Japan. She has made lots of new friends. _____
_____
_____

5. We got the new puppy. No one's shoes or socks were safe. _____
_____
_____

EXERCISE B   Combine each pair of sentences by writing one complete sentence using a connecting word such as *as, until, before, so that, if,* or *although.*

EXAMPLE **1.** Leo woke up. The alarm sounded. *Leo woke up as the*
    alarm sounded.

1. The soup boils over. Turn down the heat. _____
_____
_____

2. Take careful notes in class. You can understand them later. _____
_____
_____

Continued ☞

3. Do not remove the bread from the oven. The timer goes off. _____

_____

_____

4. Less than three percent of Hawaii's population works in agriculture. Those workers
are important to the local economy. _____

_____

_____

5. Luckily, Dad shut the gate. The pony got loose. _____

_____

_____

6. The phone call is for me. I will have to return it later. _____

_____

_____

7. We should begin cooking supper. Mom gets home from work at six o'clock. _____

_____

_____

8. I finished my homework. I should review that history chapter again. _____

_____

_____

9. We can play volleyball. It is time to baby-sit my little brother. _____

10. The puppy grows older. He will need obedience training. _____

_____

_____

LANGUAGE HANDBOOK **10** WRITING EFFECTIVE SENTENCES

WORKSHEET 11 | **Revising Wordy Sentences**

EXERCISE   Most of the following sentences are wordy. On the lines provided, revise each wordy sentence by (1) replacing a group of words with one word, (2) replacing a clause with a phrase, or (3) taking out a group of unnecessary words. If a sentence does not need improving, write *C*.

EXAMPLES 1. Mari picked up the soggy beach towels, which were very wet and full of sand. _Mari picked up the soggy, sandy_ _beach towels._

2. Mrs. Dowden, who is the sixth-grade teacher, makes learning fun. _Mrs. Dowden, the sixth-grade teacher, makes_ _learning fun._

3. The Ballet Folklorico performs Mexican dances in colorful costumes that have bright colors. _The Ballet_ _Folklorico performs Mexican dances in colorful costumes._

1. Ella painted the frame using a great deal of care and then let it dry completely. _____

_____

_____

_____

2. Because of the fact that the traffic was heavy, Mr. and Mrs. Kwan were late for the concert. _____

_____

_____

_____

3. Wednesday's softball game between the Panthers and the Colts was delayed because of rain. _____

_____

_____

_____

4. The volunteers used moist sponges, which had water on them, to wet the stamps. ____

_____

_____

_____

Continued ☞

5. Wyatt looked handsome while he was dressed in his new suit. _____

_____

_____

_____

6. Spadefoot toads use the sharp-edged growths on their hind feet for digging. _____

_____

_____

_____

7. What I am saying is that Uncle Fernando has always been a fan of golfer Lee Trevino.

_____

_____

_____

8. In spite of the fact that some bats may have rabies, most bats are harmless to people.

_____

_____

_____

9. Mr. Hartman, who is the director of the recycling program, welcomed the volunteers.

_____

_____

_____

10. The kitten had soft, fluffy fur that was soft to touch. _____

_____

_____

_____

LANGUAGE HANDBOOK **10** WRITING EFFECTIVE SENTENCES

WORKSHEET 12 | Test

EXERCISE A   On the line provided, identify each of the following word groups. Write *R* for a run-on sentence, *SF* for a sentence fragment, and *CS* for a complete sentence.

EXAMPLE ___*SF*___ **1.** Tamed the wild hawk in the ancient way.

_____ **1.** Underneath many a happy smile and a cheery face.

_____ **2.** A large bowl filled with red apples sat on the table.

_____ **3.** I can carry these boxes, they're not heavy.

_____ **4.** The mariachi band played well-known Mexican songs.

_____ **5.** My brother's room is painted yellow, mine is blue.

_____ **6.** Did you look in the encyclopedia, it's probably in there.

_____ **7.** While it was raining, we played with a jigsaw puzzle.

_____ **8.** Well, I made a promise, I'm keeping my room clean for a week.

_____ **9.** When the principal entered the auditorium for her speech.

_____ **10.** Come to my house, after dinner, we'll try my new computer program.

_____ **11.** Smashing through their defensive line for a victory.

_____ **12.** Linda hurt her knee, now she can't play ball for a while.

_____ **13.** You shouldn't have gone to so much trouble, but we certainly thank you.

_____ **14.** Most people in North Africa speak Arabic.

_____ **15.** Since that very first day at Camp Eagle in the Rockies.

_____ **16.** The Chinese writing system has nearly 50,000 characters.

_____ **17.** Our Thanksgiving turkey, shrinking a little bit day by day.

_____ **18.** It was her first ride on a train, she slept almost all the time.

_____ **19.** Australia is the sixth largest country in the world, it lies south of the equator.

_____ **20.** On the other hand, if they can't fix the telephone by Saturday morning.

_____ **21.** The falling leaves in piles all over the yard.

_____ **22.** Don't change the channel!

_____ **23.** Were at the mall on Saturday?

_____ **24.** Now that we have heard all of the candidates for office.

_____ **25.** Has he made a decision, do you agree with his ideas?

Continued ☞

EXERCISE B   The following word groups are either fragments or run-on sentences. On the lines provided, correct each fragment by adding words to make it a complete sentence. Correct each run-on sentence by separating it into two sentences.

> **EXAMPLES 1.** Considering every possible move on the chessboard. _She was_
> _considering every possible move on the chessboard._
>
> **2.** I hope you like cats, this one may crawl onto your lap. _I hope_
> _you like cats. This one may crawl onto your lap._

1. Don't eat those berries they could be poisonous! _____
_____

2. A Hopi woodcarving of the Sun Kachina, a representation of the spirit of the sun. _____
_____
_____

3. When the mist over the hills evaporated. _____
_____

4. Has that dog been in the lake again, you can wash him this time. _____
_____
_____

5. While they ran for the fire extinguisher. _____
_____

6. We have had fish every night at camp, I surely would like a change. _____
_____
_____

7. Six feet of rope should be enough, can you tie a slipknot? _____
_____

8. Just as the clock struck midnight. _____
_____

9. Imagine our surprise, a pony was eating the apples in our yard. _____
_____
_____

10. Quebec, Canada's first city and the provincial capital. _____
_____
_____

Continued ☞

LANGUAGE HANDBOOK 10 **WORKSHEET 12** (continued)

EXERCISE C   On the lines provided, combine each group of sentences by writing one complete sentence.

> **EXAMPLE 1.** A noise came from the refrigerator. The noise was strange.
> _A strange noise came from the refrigerator._

1. My grandfather gave me these tools. He gave them to me on my birthday. _____
_____
_____

2. Read me this poem. Read this poem by Gwendolyn Brooks.   _____
_____
_____

3. There are bears in this forest. The bears are dangerous. They are black bears. _____
_____
_____

4. A bitter wind blew. It was cold. It blew through the open doors. _____
_____
_____

5. We laughed. We laughed at the clown. The clown was in the circus. _____
_____
_____

EXERCISE D   On the lines provided, combine each of the following groups of sentences by using either compound subjects, compound verbs, or conjunctions.

> **EXAMPLE 1.** In the reference section are atlases. Almanacs are there, too. _In the reference section are atlases and almanacs._

1. We decided on yellow paint. Mom and Dad agreed with us. _____
_____

2. The airplane filled its tank with fuel. The airplane took off for Spain. _____
_____
_____

3. Claudia loves reading about Ali Baba and the forty thieves. So do I. _____
_____
_____

Continued ☞

4. A small tree would look nice in that corner. So would a chair. _____
_____

5. My brother could be at the bowling alley. He could be at our cousin's house. _____
_____

EXERCISE E   Combine each of the following pairs of sentences by using *as, since, when, because, if, while,* or *before*. Write your sentences on the lines provided.

> **EXAMPLE 1.** We all cheered. Natalie scored the final basket. *We all* _____
> *cheered when Natalie scored the final basket.* _____

1. Elvin can locate Saskatchewan on the map. He will win the geography bee. _____
_____
_____

2. That store opened last May. There are many more cars on the streets. _____
_____
_____

3. Save those pencils. We don't have any more. _____
_____

4. Will you peel the potatoes? I will chop the onions. _____
_____

5. The alarm clock rang. I was already awake. _____
_____

EXERCISE F   The following passage has stringy sentences. Break the passage into smaller sentences. Then, use adverbs, prepositional phrases, and connecting words to make the passage more interesting. Be sure to use correct capitalization and punctuation.

> **EXAMPLE** Roy and I went to Canada last summer, and one time we saw the
> northern lights, and the sky lit up with multicolored lights, and then
> they faded quickly. *When Roy and I went to Canada last summer, one*
> *time we saw the northern lights. In a flash, the sky lit up with*
> *multicolored lights, and then they quickly faded.*

My father and I were driving down the road last night, and we suddenly saw a strange

light in the sky, and it sped through the darkness like a shooting star, but it was very close,

Continued ☞

Writing Effective Sentences **103**

so we quickly followed it, but we could not find it, and it was getting late, so we finally

went home. _____

_____

_____

_____

_____

_____

_____

EXERCISE G Most of the sentences in the following paragraph are wordy. On the lines provided, rewrite the paragraph, revising the wordy sentences to improve the style.

> EXAMPLE [1] In the fall, which is my favorite time of year, I enjoy raking the leaves. _In the fall, my favorite time of year, I enjoy raking the leaves._

[1] At the time when most of the leaves had fallen, the whole family went to work. [2] Mom and Dad got out the yard tools known as rakes. [3] We started in the front part of the yard. [4] Mom and Timothy, who is my brother, began raking the leaves into piles. [5] When we had some nice big piles that were very large, we started filling the bags. [6] What I mean to say is that we filled more than twenty bags! [7] My little sister, whose name is Karli, even helped. [8] She grabbed handfuls of leaves in her hands and threw them into the bags. [9] Karli always seems happy to help with a family project. [10] Due to the fact that everyone helped, we were able to finish the job in just one day.

_____

_____

_____

_____

_____

_____

_____

_____

_____

LANGUAGE HANDBOOK 11 CAPITAL LETTERS

WORKSHEET 1 | Using Capital Letters

EXERCISE Circle the letters that should be capitalized in the following sentences.

EXAMPLE 1. (t)he (w)ashingtons' new cat is a calico.

1. it is a female, as are almost all calico cats.

2. janet said, "we named her ralph because that is what she says instead of meow."

3. if i ever get a cat, it will be a siamese.

4. they are good travelers, i have heard.

5. because they don't mind motion, they are often used as ships' cats.

6. my cousin has one and says, "siamese cats are more like dogs than cats."

7. his cat, named thai, likes to go on car trips.

8. armando has a dog whose breed originally came from mexico.

9. chihuahuas, named for the mexican state of chihuahua, are short-haired dogs.

10. armando says, "they are very small dogs, but they have big ears and eyes."

11. animals often are used in television, billboard, and magazine advertising.

12. pets and wild animals are also important characters in some stories and poems.

13. many books, such as *white fang,* by jack london, are about animals.

14. joseph bruchac wrote "birdfoot's grampa," a poem about frogs.

15. may sarton's poem "a parrot" starts out, "my parrot is emerald green."

16. "zlateh the goat" is a wonderful short story by isaac bashevis singer.

17. what is your favorite animal story, movie, or poem?

18. carlos says his favorite novel is *old yeller,* which is about a dog.

19. julia, who lived in kentucky on a horse farm, likes the book *black beauty*.

20. the animal movie my friend adia likes best is *babe,* which is about a pig.

21. it was filmed in australia.

22. in the movie mr. hoggett is a farmer who wins babe in a weight-guessing contest.

23. adia said, "my favorite movies are ones in which the animals talk."

24. her favorite character in *babe* is the duck named ferdinand.

25. i'm glad there are so many animal stories, poems, and movies; i'd like to read and see them all.

LANGUAGE HANDBOOK **11** **CAPITAL LETTERS**

WORKSHEET 2 **Capitalizing Proper Nouns**

EXERCISE A   For each numbered item, choose the phrase that is correctly capitalized. Write its letter on the line provided.

EXAMPLE ____*a*____ **1.** (a) Salt Lake City   (b) Salt Lake city

_____ **1.** (a) United Nations   (b) United nations

_____ **2.** (a) Bastille day   (b) Bastille Day

_____ **3.** (a) an African desert   (b) an African Desert

_____ **4.** (a) Miami Beach   (b) Miami beach

_____ **5.** (a) sunday, the first of march (b) Sunday, the first of March

_____ **6.** (a) Powder river   (b) Powder River

_____ **7.** (a) Will Rogers turnpike   (b) Will Rogers Turnpike

_____ **8.** (a) a weekend in summer   (b) a weekend in Summer

_____ **9.** (a) the Federal Trade Commission (b) the federal trade commission

_____ **10.** (a) the Pacific northwest   (b) the Pacific Northwest

EXERCISE B   Each of the following sentences contains at least one error in capitalization. Draw a line through any incorrect capital or lowercase letter, and write the correct letter above it.

EXAMPLE **1.** Did you eat in the Ꞓafeteria of the ₲uggenheim Museum?

1. My grandparents came from Manchester, england.

2. Mrs. Harrison asked everyone to attend the exhibit presented by the Fine Arts council.

3. Is your cousin still taking classes at Auburn community college?

4. In January we are going to the Sierra winter carnival at lake Tahoe.

5. Annapurna and mount Everest are two of the Mountains of the Himalayas.

6. The explorer Robert falcon Scott led an expedition to Antarctica in 1911.

7. The Boxer George Foreman has named all his sons George, jr.

8. One of the most important texts in judaism is the Talmud.

9. The most sacred city of islam is Mecca, which is in Saudi Arabia.

10. One of the most recognizable constellations in the Northern sky is the Big Dipper, also known as Ursa major.

LANGUAGE HANDBOOK 11 CAPITAL LETTERS

| WORKSHEET 3 | Capitalizing Proper Nouns |

EXERCISE A For each numbered item, choose the phrase that is correctly capitalized. Write its letter on the line provided.

EXAMPLE ___b___ 1. (a) the planet pluto (b) the planet Pluto

_____ 1. (a) the Emancipation Proclamation (b) the emancipation proclamation

_____ 2. (a) a Nissan Truck (b) a Nissan truck

_____ 3. (a) the Crusades (b) the crusades

_____ 4. (a) the earth's population (b) the Earth's Population

_____ 5. (a) made by the cherokee (b) made by the Cherokee

_____ 6. (a) the Eiffel Tower (b) the Eiffel tower

_____ 7. (a) world war I (b) World War I

_____ 8. (a) on the *titanic* (b) on the *Titanic*

_____ 9. (a) Age of Chivalry (b) age of Chivalry

_____ 10. (a) the Smithsonian institution (b) the Smithsonian Institution

EXERCISE B Each of the following sentences contains at least one error in capitalization. Draw a line through any incorrect capital or lowercase letter, and write the correct letter above it.

EXAMPLE 1. Who can name the nine planets in our ~~s~~Solar ~~s~~System?

1. A religious group we call the pilgrims came to North America on the *mayflower*.

2. This recipe calls for Pillsbury Flour.

3. During the Middle ages, few people could read.

4. American Soldiers who are wounded in battle are awarded the purple heart.

5. Have you ever crossed the Golden Gate bridge?

6. The new exchange student is from south africa.

7. A People called the berbers inhabits this desert.

8. The new church on the corner was built by a baptist congregation.

9. The battle of New Orleans was fought after the War of 1812 had officially ended.

10. While we were in Washington, D.C., we visited the national gallery of art.

LANGUAGE HANDBOOK 11 CAPITAL LETTERS

WORKSHEET 4 | **Capitalizing Proper Adjectives and School Subjects**

EXERCISE Most of the following sentences contain at least one word that should be capitalized. Draw a line through any incorrect words. Then, on the line provided, write the word or words correctly. If a sentence is already correct, write *C*.

EXAMPLE _____Mexican_____ **1.** Is this really the first time that you have eaten ~~mexican~~ food?

_____ **1.** My hungarian grandfather will visit us in July.

_____ **2.** I'm late for french class.

_____ **3.** She showed slides of her European trip.

_____ **4.** I am taking metalworking II next year.

_____ **5.** We're having a hawaiian luau tonight.

_____ **6.** What is the jeffersonian idea of democracy?

_____ **7.** I'm wearing my dutch shoes to the Folk Fair.

_____ **8.** Read the chapter on italian customs.

_____ **9.** What is the largest north american animal?

_____ **10.** David's best subjects are Spanish and health II.

_____ **11.** Many of the ancient greek plays are still performed.

_____ **12.** Sibelius is a famous Finnish composer.

_____ **13.** Most austrian farmers grow sugar beets and potatoes.

_____ **14.** The people on the farm next to ours raise arabian horses.

_____ **15.** My favorite classes are russian and math.

_____ **16.** The swedish language is spoken by nine million people.

_____ **17.** Around the world, panama hats are famous for their high quality.

_____ **18.** Do you eat your tests in home economics II?

_____ **19.** Let's play a game of chinese checkers.

_____ **20.** Is that a Persian rug?

_____ **21.** Where can you find good thai food in Boston?

_____ **22.** We are studying african american authors this semester.

_____ **23.** Did you read about the Spanish-American War in your Spanish class?

_____ **24.** My mother drives an old british sports car.

_____ **25.** Some indian curries are very spicy.

LANGUAGE
HANDBOOK **11** **CAPITAL LETTERS**

WORKSHEET 5 | **Capitalizing Titles**

EXERCISE   In the following sentences, draw a line through each incorrect capital or lowercase letter and write the correct letter above it.

EXAMPLE **1.** *Brighty Øf Ṫhe Grand Ċanyon* is a book about a burro.

1. Are those copies of *Popular computing* still on the table?

2. Give the order for the charge, captain!

3. The prince of Wales is the title of the male who will become king of England.

4. Pictures of famous writers are displayed on the walls of the library, professor.

5. Ask your Doctor about a good exercise program.

6. The old television program featured president Bush.

7. My Aunt Margie is running for judge in our county.

8. Jody and Grandpa are watching a rerun of *Father knows Best*.

9. Did you understand the poem "The Rime Of The Ancient Mariner"?

10. Tell us, sheriff Fielder, about your approach to solving crime.

11. I'm playing one of the children in *The sound of music*.

12. *The Cavalry Charge on the southern Plains* is one of Frederic Remington's most exciting paintings.

13. My Mother and Father met when they were in college.

14. Unfortunately, the book *then again, maybe i won't* was checked out at the library.

15. Alana's story is titled "One day at the beach."

16. The march "Pomp and circumstance No. 1" is played at graduations every year.

17. My favorite song in the musical *The king and I* is "getting to know you."

18. The President of the French Club turned in the forms yesterday.

19. I am reading an article about secretary of state Madeleine Albright.

20. We have to memorize "Jimmy Jet and His TV set" for English class.

21. President Lincoln wrote the Gettysburg address to commemorate the dedication of a cemetery at Gettysburg, Pennsylvania.

22. The Minister of our church is pastor Lewis.

23. Do you know the motto of *the New York times*?

24. We saw senator John Glenn on *meet the press* this morning.

25. One of my uncle's favorite plays is *I Never Sang For My Father*.

LANGUAGE HANDBOOK	**11**	CAPITAL LETTERS

WORKSHEET 6	Test

EXERCISE A   Each of the following sentences contains at least one word that should be capitalized. Draw a line through any incorrect words. Then, on the line provided, write the word or words correctly.

EXAMPLE _____Irish_____ **1.** Of all dogs, I like ~~irish~~ setters most.

_____ **1.** Will governor Martinez give his speech before the luncheon?

_____ **2.** During the Civil War some Union troops were from the south.

_____ **3.** Is grandfather superintendent of that building?

_____ **4.** Was your mother a naval officer, walt?

_____ **5.** Who do you think will win the Rose bowl this year?

_____ **6.** We're picking up a vessel on radar, captain.

_____ **7.** Mark Twain was the author of *Life on the mississippi*.

_____ **8.** This cuban bread is delicious.

_____ **9.** The article called "Raising pigeons for Profit" is in last month's issue.

_____ **10.** My parents frequently speak spanish at home.

EXERCISE B   Each of the following sentences contains at least one word that should not be capitalized. Draw a line through any incorrect words. Then, on the line provided, write the word or words correctly.

EXAMPLE _____computer_____ **1.** We programmed the Compuquick ~~Computer~~ to play checkers.

_____ **1.** The Secretary of the Science Club will take the minutes.

_____ **2.** Do you have a replacement cord for a Defuzzer Razor?

_____ **3.** Representatives from several Faiths were present at the conference.

_____ **4.** Is Uncle Ted teaching that course in Home Economics?

_____ **5.** This Winter, Zachary Taylor Middle School will move.

_____ **6.** The classrooms for History II and Typing are crowded.

_____ **7.** Let's stay at a Motel right on Myrtle Beach!

_____ **8.** Under the bright rays of the Sun, the Seafood Festival began.

_____ **9.** All the Schools send students to the New England Science Center.

_____ **10.** The Greeks once believed that the Gods lived on Mount Olympus.

Continued ☞

EXERCISE C Proofread the following sentences for correct capitalization. Some words are incorrectly capitalized, and some words that should be capitalized are not. Draw a line through any incorrect letter, and write the correct letter above it.

      EXAMPLE 1. Evenings, especially ~~f~~riday evenings, are for ~~F~~amily at the Walters' house.

1. Are we going to the Mountains for your birthday in november?

2. Does anyone ever ring the liberty bell?

3. Mesa Verde national Park features the homes of cliff dwellers.

4. We placed a wreath on the Tomb of the Unknown soldier.

5. On the front steps sat bill and his brother.

6. Direct your questions to the house of Representatives in Washington, D.C.

7. Please do not make me sing "the Twelve days of Christmas" again.

8. Before you can take Swimming, you need your doctor's permission.

9. The spacecraft went past saturn into the farthest reaches of our solar system.

10. Isn't Labor day always on a monday?

11. Didn't doctor Harmon tell you to get a tetanus shot before you go to camp balcones?

12. John Hancock was the first person to sign the Declaration of independence.

13. Surely you have heard of the battle of Britain.

14. At eight o'clock, the President of the company addressed the audience.

15. The *hindenburg* disaster held back the development of dirigible airships.

16. What was one result of World war I?

17. Hillside methodist Church is up the hill from the park.

18. I watched a rerun of *the Beverly hillbillies*.

19. A Department Store is having a big sale downtown.

20. After we toured the pacific northwest, we headed south for Los angeles.

21. Call This Week for reservations at the Campground!

22. tomorrow, i will be working on props for our skit "the mice."

23. Fran asked her Aunt Emily to play a mystery Board Game with us.

24. will dr. Cabot have time to give me an Eye Exam today?

25. Let's have Maureen sing an irish song at our Recital.

LANGUAGE HANDBOOK 12 PUNCTUATION

WORKSHEET 1 | **Using End Marks**

EXERCISE   For each of the following sentences, insert an appropriate end mark and periods where they are needed for abbreviations.

EXAMPLE **1.** Mrs. West has an appointment this afternoon.

1. What on earth is going on here

2. Have you met Dr Mendez, our new neighbor

3. Please eat your rice more slowly

4. Here comes the first float

5. Have you read the work of the poet E E Cummings

6. Were you at the soccer game last night

7. Notice the delicate structure of these leaves

8. Get that dog out of here right now

9. Connie hurried to the gym after school

10. We called and called, but no one answered

11. Color all graphs and charts in your science workbook

12. Could Mr O'Sullivan drive us to the Hill School Science Fair

13. Meet Mom and me at 3:00 P M by the pier

14. The library has several books on Scandinavian cultures

15. Keep away from the edge of the pool

16. Did you give the report on aboriginal peoples to Ms Alexander

17. Our dog can sit up, roll over, and fetch the paper

18. Watch out for that puddle

19. Please pass me the bread

20. Did you know that a suslik is a type of squirrel found in Europe and Asia

21. Tell me what you learned in class today

22. Do you know whether we have any yogurt

23. Everyone took the day off and went to the beach

24. Don't drop that vase

25. The movie is about the British adventurer T E Lawrence

LANGUAGE HANDBOOK 12 PUNCTUATION

WORKSHEET 2 | **Using Commas to Separate Items in a Series**

EXERCISE A In each of the following sentences, insert commas where they are needed.

> **EXAMPLE** 1. Winter, spring, summer, and fall are the four seasons of the year.

1. On our hike we saw a fox a quail and a horned toad.

2. Bring an atlas a dictionary a pen and a blank sheet of paper.

3. The puppy searched for his toy behind the sofa under the bed and in the magazine rack.

4. My new futon is wide soft and very comfortable.

5. Swans ducks and geese flocked to the children for bread crumbs.

6. People visited the Great Wall of China in buses on foot and on bicycles.

7. Beans and rice ham and eggs and fresh fish are some favorite foods for campers.

8. I stayed with Monsieur Durand his wife and their children when I visited Quebec.

9. I know that Derrick David or Djuna will set the table.

10. Mom said not to forget our thank-you notes to Uncle Eli Grandma and Grandpa.

EXERCISE B For each of the following sentences, correct errors in the use of commas. Write the sentence on the line provided, inserting or leaving out commas as needed. If a sentence is already correct, write *C*.

> **EXAMPLES** 1. Lani and Irene and Josh and Kane were all there. _C_
>
> 2. A good friend should be loyal trustworthy and polite. _A_
>   _good friend should be loyal, trustworthy, and polite._

1. Mr. Nakai is teaching the Navajo language to Elena Greg and me. _____

_____

2. Either my brother my older sister or my best friend will bowl with me. _____

_____

3. Ms. Day said that Ben Stephanie and Alicia will be partners. _____

_____

4. The computer beeped, displayed a message, and flashed a red light. _____

_____

5. Did you see Danny, or his mother, or his sister at the Bakers' house? _____

_____

LANGUAGE HANDBOOK **12** **PUNCTUATION**

| WORSHEET 3 | Using Commas to Separate Adjectives and the Parts of Compound Sentences |

EXERCISE A   In the following sentences, insert commas where they are needed.

> **EXAMPLES 1.** We drank cold, clear water from the well.
>
> **2.** I have never been to Italy, but maybe I'll go someday.

1. Some plants like the shade but others need sunlight.

2. The trip to Antarctica was long and dangerous but Admiral Byrd succeeded in his goal.

3. There were hard feelings on all sides yet everyone agreed to a compromise.

4. A soft pencil produces a fuzzy dark line.

5. In the back seat of the car was a litter of hungry noisy impatient puppies.

6. David and I bought Dad a present and we hid it in the cluttered dusty attic.

7. Thick sooty dark smoke was coming from the chimney.

8. Your reports on the Central American rain forests are due on Monday but you may hand them in on Friday.

9. I was wrong but we all make mistakes.

10. The program started to boot but the screen suddenly went blank.

EXERCISE B   On the lines provided, copy each of the following sentences, inserting commas as needed. If a sentence is already correct, write *C*.

> **EXAMPLE 1.** You may mow the lawn or you may sweep the driveway.
>
> <u>You may mow the lawn, or you may sweep the driveway.</u>

1. Javier likes to read the newspaper, and he hopes to be a reporter some day. _____

   _____

2. What are these wet muddy boots doing in the front hall? _____

   _____

3. New Zealand is made up of two large narrow islands. _____

   _____

4. On the steps was a small box with a wide shiny red ribbon. _____

   _____

5. The power is turned on but the machine still will not work. _____

   _____

LANGUAGE HANDBOOK 12 PUNCTUATION

WORKSHEET 4 | Using Commas with Interrupters

EXERCISE A   Each of the following sentences contains an expression that interrupts the sentence. Insert commas where they are needed. If a sentence is already correct, write *C* on the line provided.

EXAMPLE _____ **1.** The answer to your question, Diana, is right in the book.

_____ **1.** New Guinea the world's second-largest island is in the Pacific.

_____ **2.** No you may not ride your bicycle all the way across town.

_____ **3.** Is your skateboard in the garage Sabrina?

_____ **4.** Our teacher a professional dancer showed us the steps.

_____ **5.** We girls, the Jets soccer team, use the field between 4:00 and 5:00 P.M.

_____ **6.** Willie have you seen Emilio in the building?

_____ **7.** Why what a lovely surprise this is!

_____ **8.** Wisconsin a leading dairy producer is known for its cheeses.

_____ **9.** Well you certainly are feeling better!

_____ **10.** A Chinese junk Lisa is a type of sailboat.

EXERCISE B   Proofread the following sentences for correct use of commas with interrupters. Insert commas where they are needed. If a sentence is already correct, write *C* on the line provided.

EXAMPLE _____ **1.** Ask Mom's friend, an excellent seamstress, about your hem.

_____ **1.** Hong Kong a major commercial center is located in Southeast Asia.

_____ **2.** My what a fine bicycle you have there Teddy!

_____ **3.** Lance we do have an opening in the computer class.

_____ **4.** My youngest sister Edith is entering her drawings in the state fair this year.

_____ **5.** You may use the old typewriter the one in the blue case.

_____ **6.** The second *Star Wars* film *The Empire Strikes Back* is my favorite.

_____ **7.** May I help you across the street Sir?

_____ **8.** Why how did you know it was my birthday?

_____ **9.** His brother Tom picked out the gift, but his brother Mike paid for it.

_____ **10.** Jada please bring me your plate.

| WORKSHEET 5 | **Using Commas in Dates, Addresses, and Letters** |

EXERCISE A   Insert commas where they are needed.

> **EXAMPLE 1.** Carol received this letter on September 5, 2000.

August 31 2000

Ms. Carol Metcalfe

507 Seymour Street

Ann Arbor MI 48104

Dear Ms. Metcalfe:

   Thank you for your letter of Thursday August 17 2000. I'm afraid we do not have in stock the book you are trying to find. According to *Publishers Weekly* of September 19 1996, *The Wild Colonial Boy* was taken out of print by its publisher. You might be able to find it at a used book store. We recommend Benton Fraser Books, at 24 Mackenzie Street Toronto Ontario Canada. We also recommend Loon Feather Bookshop, at 853 Anderson Avenue Viola KS 67149. Since the story takes place in Ireland and England, you might also try bookshops in Dublin Ireland or London England. Since any of these places might have to search for a copy of the book, you might not be able to purchase it before your father's birthday on September 13 2000.

Sincerely yours

Linda Marciano

EXERCISE B   Proofread the following sentences for errors in punctuation, inserting commas where they are needed.

> **EXAMPLE 1.** They will arrive on Flight 44 on Saturday, November 23.

1. Gina once lived in Phoenix Arizona.

2. The ship is bound for San Juan Puerto Rico.

3. Send the package to 452 North Cedar St. Pittsburgh Pennsylvania.

4. Is the test on Friday November 5 or Friday November 12?

5. The letter in the trunk was postmarked January 3 1916.

LANGUAGE HANDBOOK **12** **PUNCTUATION**

WORKSHEET 6 | **Using Semicolons and Colons**

EXERCISE A   In each of the following sentences, insert semicolons and colons wherever they are needed.

> **EXAMPLE 1.** You were right; my boots were in the hall closet.

1. The return address should include the following information your name, street address, city, state, and ZIP Code.

2. Belize is located along the Caribbean coast of Central America it used to be called British Honduras.

3. Kelly will be ready at 3 00 P.M., and Nicole will be here ten minutes earlier.

4. My brother has a turtle for a pet my sister has a boa constrictor.

5. Ms. Sakamoto wants to talk to you she heard about your idea for a chess tournament.

6. Every camper should have everything on this list a compass, a sleeping bag, a good pair of shoes, and a change of clothes.

7. This book on American Indians is worth reading you can check it out from the library.

8. It's only 8 30 P.M. we have time for a crossword game.

9. My teacher suggested that I read *Lives and Moments An Introduction to Short Fiction*.

10. Which of the following states is famous for its redwood trees Massachusetts, Rhode Island, California, or Hawaii?

EXERCISE B   On the line provided, rewrite each sentence and punctuate it correctly with colons or semicolons.

> **EXAMPLE 1.** The three primary colors of paint are the following red, yellow, and blue. *The three primary colors of paint are the following: red, yellow, and blue.*

1. There are no wheels on this vehicle it uses an air cushion instead. _____

   _____

2. You will need these items a wrench, a screwdriver, and a pair of pliers. _____

   _____

3. Be there early no one will be admitted after 7 30 P.M. _____

   _____

4. Uruguay is in South America it borders Brazil and Argentina. _____

   _____

5. We cleaned the following rooms the living room, the kitchen, and the porch. _____

   _____

LANGUAGE HANDBOOK 12 PUNCTUATION

WORKSHEET 7 | **Test**

EXERCISE A   Supply the proper end mark for each of the following sentences. Correctly punctuate any abbreviations.

EXAMPLES **1.** Have you seen Ms. Baker this morning**?**

2. Mail this card to P.O. Box 472, Del Rio, TX 78841**.**

1. I finished my report on Bora-Bora

2. Is that the only shirt in your closet

3. Don't ever wake me up at 3:00 A M again

4. Mr Norton has not finished with the projector

5. Did you know that the original settlers of Hawaii were Polynesians

6. Run for your lives

7. He lives at 1600 North Clark St, Chicago, Ill

8. What a beautiful rainbow that is

9. Tell me about yourself, Ms Wong

10. Just look at how much you've grown

EXERCISE B   In the following sentences, insert commas where they are needed.

EXAMPLE **1.** Well**,** I'm not going on that roller coaster**,** and that's final.

1. Our cat a purebred Siamese can sometimes be a little nervous.

2. I have tickets for Ricardo Nick and Paolo to the Ballet Folklorico on Saturday March 3.

3. Mrs. Park this is my youngest cousin Ellen from Erie Pennsylvania.

4. We read the recipe measured out the ingredients and mixed them in a large bowl.

5. No you may not use my hair dryer on the dog.

6. Our pilot was helpful courteous and skillful.

7. An extra hour's work wouldn't hurt you Damon.

8. Mom Kim borrowed my tapes but he didn't bring them back.

9. A big old thick envelope with my name on it lay on the table.

10. They dropped anchor in the Gulf of Honduras and everyone went for a swim.

Continued ☞

EXERCISE C   On each line provided, write the letter of the correctly punctuated salutation or closing.

		A	B
EXAMPLE	_B_	1. Dear Dad:	Dear Dad,

		A	B
_____	1.	To Whom It May Concern:	To Whom It May Concern,
_____	2.	Dear Senator Ogata,	Dear Senator Ogata:
_____	3.	Dear Aunt Alani:	Dear Aunt Alani,
_____	4.	Gentlemen:	Gentlemen,
_____	5.	Yours truly:	Yours truly,

EXERCISE D   In each of the following sentences, insert a semicolon or colon wherever it is needed.

EXAMPLES   1. Please bring the following: paintbrushes, aprons, and gloves.
2. I will leave home today; I'll try to be there by tomorrow evening.

1. The alarm was set for 6 30 A.M. but went off at 4 00 A.M.

2. We planted tomatoes in April we've had fresh tomatoes all summer.

3. The new social studies unit focuses on the writing and speeches of the following American Indians Sarah Winnemucca, Tecumseh, and Pontiac.

4. Does the meeting start at 7 30 or 7 45 P.M.?

5. We need to get there early we are doing a presentation.

6. Have you read *Amistad Rising The Story of Freedom* by Veronica Chambers?

7. Summer vacation will be fun I'm going to baseball camp.

8. The mural in the art room is done mostly in the following colors orange, purple, and red.

9. If you like biographies, you will enjoy *A Brilliant Streak The Making of Mark Twain*.

10. My brother's birthday is tomorrow we're surprising him with a trip to the beach.

Continued ☞

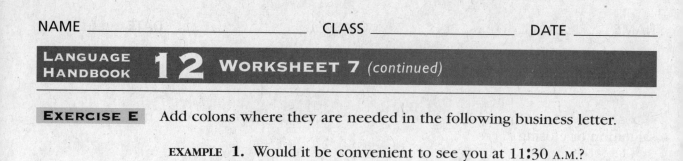

EXERCISE E   Add colons where they are needed in the following business letter.

> **EXAMPLE 1.** Would it be convenient to see you at 11:30 A.M.?

Dear Senator Cruz

Our class has read your book for students *A New America The Advantages of a Multicultural Society*. We are impressed with your ideas and goals. Every Wednesday from 9 45 to 10 15 A.M., we discuss your ideas for bettering our school and community.

We understand that in May you will visit our area. It would be an honor to hear you present your ideas in a speech at our school assembly either on May 3 at 2 30 P.M. or on May 10 at 1 45 P.M. Please let us know if either time will fit into your schedule. We understand that your latest book, *Reaching Out Ten Steps to a Better Community,* will soon be published. If you have time, we would appreciate a question-and-answer session with you about it from 3 00 to 3 30 P.M. on the day you speak.

We look forward to hearing from you.

Sincerely,

The sixth-grade class at Elmwood Middle School

LANGUAGE HANDBOOK	**13** PUNCTUATION

WORKSHEET 1 | Using Italics and Quotation Marks in Titles

EXERCISE A   In the following sentences, underline each title that should be in italics.

> EXAMPLE 1. Have you read the latest issue of the magazine <u>National Geographic</u>?

1. Was Mary Shelley the author of the novel Frankenstein?

2. One of the most famous ships in Western mythology is the Argo, Jason's sailing vessel.

3. We put a classified ad in the East Side News.

4. Edith Hamilton's book Mythology will tell you all about the Greek gods and goddesses.

5. Of all the paintings at the museum, I liked Water Lilies by Claude Monet most.

6. Every night after dinner, Nicoletta and Jackie watch Kratts' Creatures on PBS.

7. Perhaps the most famous work of the Russian composer Igor Stravinsky is The Rite of Spring.

8. My mom still has her old vinyl copy of the Beatles album Abbey Road.

9. This year the drama club is staging a production of The Music Man.

10. Return of the Jedi is my favorite movie.

EXERCISE B   In the following sentences, put quotation marks at the beginning and end of each title that should be enclosed in quotation marks.

> EXAMPLE 1. My favorite short story is "Rappacini's Daughter."

1. Who will sing The Star-Spangled Banner at the World Series?

2. The January issue of this science magazine has an article called Scientist of the Year.

3. The article Making Your Own Patterns includes several helpful hints for the beginner.

4. The third chapter, The Norman Conquest, is interesting.

5. Let Tamika read Countee Cullen's poem Tableau.

6. Mrs. Long assigned us the short story The Gold Cadillac.

7. The first episode of *Star Trek: The Next Generation* is Encounter at Farpoint.

8. At the concert last night I heard John Fogerty sing his song Down on the Corner.

9. One of the poems in the book is Steam Shovel by Charles Malam.

10. Is The Emperor's New Clothes the first short story Tom remembers reading?

| LANGUAGE HANDBOOK | 13 | PUNCTUATION |

WORKSHEET 2 | **Punctuating Quotations and Titles**

EXERCISE A   In each of the following sentences, insert quotation marks and other punctuation where needed. Draw a line through lowercase letters that should be capitalized, and write the correct uppercase letters above them.

EXAMPLE   1.   Carl asked, "ᴰdid Dad say that we could stay out late?"

1. Ms. Platero said Never smell a strange chemical!

2. Do you remember where Siberia is located the teacher asked.

3. Don't sit in Dad's new chair my friend cautioned.

4. Congress Mr. Sánchez said is responsible for making laws.

5. The meeting will begin the secretary stated at three o'clock.

6. Who said be there an hour early?

7. A good rider she said does not need spurs.

8. Will you water my plants my sister asked.

9. Ms. Mack said today, we will read poetry by Lucha Corpi.

10. Watch out yelled the police officer.

EXERCISE B   Insert the commas and single and double quotation marks that have been omitted from the following sentences. If a sentence is already correct, write *C* on the line provided.

EXAMPLE   _____   1.   "Have you read the story 'Raymond's Run'?" asked Abdul.

_____   1. Who wants to go to a movie? asked Ella.

_____   2. Here said Carlos let me help you with that.

_____   3. The title of my story is Betsy's Secret said Lisa.

_____   4. Otto told us that his sister was coming home from college.

_____   5. My mother wrote the article Hispanic Chamber of Commerce Honors Students in yesterday's paper said Frieda.

_____   6. Honey catches more flies than vinegar stated Mrs. Hofer.

_____   7. My grandmother often says that a penny saved is a penny earned.

_____   8. Can you help me? asked the driver. I need to get to the post office.

_____   9. What a terrific meal! said my mother.

_____   10. The mail carrier exclaimed Beware of the dog!

LANGUAGE HANDBOOK 13 PUNCTUATION

| WORKSHEET 3 | **Using Quotation Marks**

EXERCISE A   Add punctuation marks and single and double quotation marks where they are needed in the following sentences.

EXAMPLE **1.** Katerina asked, "May we please sing 'Red River Valley' first?"

1. I think Francisco Jiménez's short story The Circuit is very sad said Terri.

2. It is sad said Marcus and it is a true depiction of the life of migrant workers.

3. My mother and uncle were brought up in a family that did that kind of work, he added.

4. The first piece of piano music many people learn is Row, Row, Row Your Boat.

5. Araba said, Do we really have to memorize a long poem to recite to the class

6. If so she said I want to memorize The Highwayman by Alfred Noyes.

7. Wow! What a great poem exclaimed Constance.

8. Did Mr. Lee say Write a short story

9. Ronald replied Mr. Lee said Write a short poem.

10. Be sure to bring your permission slips. You should also bring your lunches. We'll meet in the school parking lot Saturday morning at eight said Coach Ward.

EXERCISE B   Punctuate the following dialogue correctly. Use a paragraph sign (¶) to show where a new paragraph should begin.

EXAMPLE "What have you been doing?" Angie asked Carlos. ¶ "I've been in the library," he said, "almost all afternoon."

I just read an article about the common cold in *Reader's Digest*, said Carlos. It's called Surprising Facts About the Common Cold. Boy, was I surprised! What are some of the facts asked Angie. I think I'm getting a cold. Well, Carlos replied, heavy clothing doesn't prevent colds. Neither does vitamin C. Plenty of rest and a well-balanced diet are the best treatments for a cold. Angie said My mother always says Drink plenty of fluids. So does the article said Carlos.

LANGUAGE HANDBOOK 13 PUNCTUATION

WORKSHEET 4 | Test

EXERCISE A Punctuate the following sentences, using underlining, single and double quotation marks, and other marks of punctuation as needed. If speakers change in an item, use a paragraph sign (¶) to show where a new paragraph should begin.

EXAMPLE 1. "Are we going to see Air Bud?" asked Derek. ¶ "When does the movie start?" asked Jon.

1. LaTanya said The first poem I ever memorized was Harlem by Langston Hughes.

2. The hurricane said the meteorologist is stalled on the Georgia coast.

3. Look out shouted Craig.

4. Was the article A Four-Day School Week in yesterday's paper asked Eduardo.

5. Did you enjoy reading Mark Twain's book The Adventures of Tom Sawyer asked Annette. Yes said Louis and I also liked his short story The Celebrated Jumping Frog of Calaveras County.

6. I am taking flute lessons said Hana and want to learn to play Londonderry Air.

7. Have you heard of the twelve-hour-long Russian movie of the book War and Peace asked Inga.

8. Mom asked Isn't it Gary's turn to wash the dishes reported Deanna.

9. My favorite episode of the TV program Nature said Wyatt is Extraordinary Dogs.

10. The atlas in our classroom is out of date said Keung. It shows Beijing with its old name, *Peking*.

EXERCISE B Punctuate the following sentences, using underlining, quotation marks, and other marks of punctuation as needed. If speakers change in an item, use a paragraph sign (¶) to show where a new paragraph should begin.

EXAMPLE 1. "Where is the issue of Ceramics Monthly that was here in the art room?" Cindy asked. ¶ Carlos answered, "I took it home by mistake and forgot to bring it back."

1. We could make piñatas for our Cinco de Mayo party said Ms. Morales but we'd need to start this week.

2. Kelly said I have a wonderful book by George Ancona called The Piñata Maker—El Piñatero. It gives detailed instructions in English and Spanish for making piñatas.

3. How great exclaimed Ms. Morales. Could you please bring it to class tomorrow

Continued ☞

4. Meanwhile, may we start on some design ideas today asked Todd. That's a good idea, said Ms. Morales.

5. Let's play the Best of Mexico CD while we work, said Ingrid.

6. What are your favorite songs on it asked Lizzie. Mine are Guadalajara and Estrellita.

7. I really prefer the La Bamba soundtrack CD, said Monty, but I like this one, too.

8. Since we need newspapers for the piñatas, it's a good thing we haven't recycled the copies of the Morning Tribune, said Kelly.

9. Before we tear up yesterday's paper, please cut out the Best Poetry Books of the Year article. I want to post it in the library, said Ms. Morales.

10. Maybe one of us should write a song called The Piñata Makers about our project laughed Shelly.

EXERCISE C   Punctuate the following sentences, using underlining, single and double quotation marks, and other marks of punctuation as needed. If speakers change in an item, use a paragraph sign (¶) to show where a new paragraph should begin.

EXAMPLE 1. "Are you familiar with Winslow Homer's watercolor The Pumpkin Patch?" asked Jerold. ¶ "I don't remember that painting," said Ron.

1. Yes, said Kala and I like the blurred colors in it.

2. Well, I prefer the bright colors in other artists' work, such as Romare Bearden's great painting Le Jazz, said Bettina.

3. I read a magazine article called Romare Bearden: Harlem Renaissance Master said Javier It was very interesting.

4. Strong colors are used in the work of many artists, said Mr. Towne, such as the great Mexican muralist Diego Rivera and the French artist Henri Matisse. In fact, Matisse wrote text and created brightly colored art for a book called Jazz.

5. My favorite artworks are drawings, said Jonathan. Mine too, said Lian, and what I like best are the pictures James Thurber drew to go with his stories.

6. His dogs are so funny looking exclaimed Francine.

7. Have you read Thurber's book Fables for Our Time asked Melanie.

8. Yes said Justin and I love the story The Fairly Intelligent Fly. It teaches that groups are not always right.

9. The drawings that go with the story What Happened to Charles look simple said Kwame, yet the animals have really great expressions.

10. Yikes shouted Michel. We've talked through our entire class time.

Continued ☞

EXERCISE D Punctuate the following sentences, using underlining, single and double quotation marks, and other marks of punctuation. If speakers change in an item, use a paragraph sign (¶) to show where a new paragraph should begin. Draw a line through each lowercase letter that should be capitalized, and write the correct uppercase letter above it.

EXAMPLES 1. "Did you see the movie <u>The Parent Trap</u>?" asked Kim.
"It's about twins whose parents are divorced."

2. "We just heard the final score," announced Sylvia. ¶
"Wasn't it great to win the first game!" exclaimed Darwin.

1. Recently I read the book Hang a Thousand Trees with Ribbons by Ann Rinaldi, said Hunter. it's the story of Phillis Wheatley.

2. Oh yes said Maryanne she's the young girl from West Africa who was sold into slavery. She later was educated by the Wheatley family and became a poet.

3. Please read the poem Trade Winds by John Masefield said Ms. Conner.

4. Hooray exclaimed Jennifer. the school band will compete in the finals. Yes, said Mitch, and we're practicing the pieces America the Beautiful and Colonel Bogey March for the competition.

5. Did you get the recipe for corn bread from that Southern Living magazine article Southern Quick Breads asked Lily.

6. The title of my poem said Nathan is The Cactus in the Teacup.

7. The mail was late yesterday said Adela but it's early today.

8. We rode the train called The Sunset Limited, said Adowa.

9. What else do we need for the vegetable curry that we're fixing Tracy asked.

10. Erin and Kathy said Phil will sing Summertime as a duet in the talent show.

LANGUAGE HANDBOOK **14** PUNCTUATION

WORKSHEET 1 | Using Apostrophes to Show Possession

EXERCISE A   In the appropriate columns, write the singular possessive and the plural possessive of each noun listed below.

	SINGULAR		PLURAL
EXAMPLE **1.** puppy	_puppy's_	puppies	_puppies'_
1. mouse	_____	mice	_____
2. girl	_____	girls	_____
3. ox	_____	oxen	_____
4. box	_____	boxes	_____
5. woman	_____	women	_____
6. pony	_____	ponies	_____
7. pyramid	_____	pyramids	_____
8. gentleman	_____	gentlemen	_____
9. child	_____	children	_____
10. elf	_____	elves	_____
11. country	_____	countries	_____
12. tortilla	_____	tortillas	_____
13. kangaroo	_____	kangaroos	_____
14. hamster	_____	hamsters	_____
15. immigrant	_____	immigrants	_____
16. neighbor	_____	neighbors	_____
17. firefighter	_____	firefighters	_____
18. baby	_____	babies	_____
19. boss	_____	bosses	_____
20. camel	_____	camels	_____
21. shelf	_____	shelves	_____
22. radio	_____	radios	_____
23. dish	_____	dishes	_____
24. goose	_____	geese	_____
25. rainbow	_____	rainbows	_____

Continued ☞

EXERCISE B   On the line provided, rewrite each of the following expressions, using the possessive case.

>   EXAMPLE **1.** the cat belonging to the Davises
>   *the Davises' cat* _____

1. the capital of Kenya

_____

2. the books belonging to Nancy

_____

3. the ring belonging to Grandfather

_____

4. the cunning of the fox

_____

5. the car belonging to Ms. Terry

_____

EXERCISE C   In each of the following sentences, underline the correct form of the italicized pronouns in parentheses.

>   EXAMPLE **1.** Those are (*his'*, *his*) autographed baseballs.

1. The steel drum music turned out to be (*everyone's, everyones*) favorite.

2. Gwendolyn Brooks is a great poet; my favorite poems are (*her's, hers*).

3. Are these flower seeds (*your's, yours*)?

4. Huynh Quang Nhuong often writes about (*his', his*) former home in Vietnam.

5. When will we find out which recycling bin is (*our's, ours*)?

6. It must be the green one because the blue one is (*their's, theirs*).

7. It is (*no one's, no ones*) fault that the game was postponed.

8. The cat enjoys using (*it's, its*) scratching post almost as much it enjoys using the side of the couch.

9. The backpack left in the locker room could be (*anyone's, anyones*).

10. (*Somebody's, Somebodys*) science project just ate a hole in the table.

LANGUAGE HANDBOOK **14** **PUNCTUATION**

| WORSHEET 2 | Using Apostrophes in Contractions and Plurals

EXERCISE A   On the line provided, write the contraction for each of the following pairs of words.

EXAMPLE **1.** it is _____*it's*_____

1. will not   _____   **11.** we will   _____

2. I am   _____   **12.** they would _____

3. car is   _____   **13.** have not   _____

4. you are   _____   **14.** she will   _____

5. let us   _____   **15.** they have   _____

6. do not   _____   **16.** should not _____

7. who is   _____   **17.** could not   _____

8. has not   _____   **18.** 1998   _____

9. were not   _____   **19.** are not   _____

10. does not _____   **20.** they are   _____

EXERCISE B   On the line provided, write and punctuate correctly any italicized word or letter in the following sentences that requires an apostrophe. If a sentence contains no apostrophe error, write *C*.

EXAMPLE _____*thank-you's*_____ **1.** A few *thank-you*s count for a lot.

_____ **1.** Make your *a*s carefully, so they won't look like *e*s.

_____ **2.** You should avoid using too many *so*'s in your writing.

_____ **3.** *Whos* going to the game on Friday evening?

_____ **4.** Yes, *Ill* be happy to entertain Mrs. Jackson's twins.

_____ **5.** *Whats* the command to exit this program?

_____ **6.** You *wouldnt* be teasing me, would you?

_____ **7.** No, *were* going to Mexico this summer.

_____ **8.** Sam, *its* time for someone to give the dog a bath, and you're elected.

_____ **9.** Aha! *Heres* the trick to this experiment.

_____ **10.** Luckily, I *didn't* lose the pictures we took in Canada.

LANGUAGE
HANDBOOK **14 PUNCTUATION**

| WORKSHEET 3 | Using Apostrophes in Contractions and Plurals

EXERCISE A   On the line provided, write the contraction for the italicized words in each of the following sentences.

EXAMPLE   _____*Where's*_____   1. *Where is* Saratoga Springs on this map of New York?

_____   1. People who *have not* read Joseph Bruchac's writing are missing a treat.

_____   2. His American Indian stories and poems *should not* be overlooked.

_____   3. *There is* much to be learned from them about respecting the earth.

_____   4. *We would* like to start an environmental club here at school.

_____   5. *I am* speaking to different classes about it.

_____   6. So far, there *are not* any people opposed to the idea.

_____   7. We *will not* wait until next year to start.

_____   8. *Let us* all join together to cut down on waste and pollution now.

_____   9. A planning meeting will be held next Wednesday at three *of the clock*.

_____ 10. I *cannot* think of anything that would keep me from attending the meeting.

EXERCISE B   Add apostrophes where they are needed in the following sentences.

EXAMPLE 1. Did you dot all of the *i*'s in that word?

1. *X*s can be used as signatures by people who cannot write their names.

2. Her phone number has three *5*s and two *3*s.

3. Don't forget to add *!*s to those exclamatory sentences.

4. Usually people say many *ah*s when they see a live panda.

5. All of the *remember*s on that poster should be underlined.

6. Don't put *≠*s in those problems; the numbers are to be subtracted.

7. Do *?*s go inside or outside quotation marks?

8. There are not enough *thank-you*s in that letter.

9. His speech would have been better without all the *uh*s.

10. It's better to write out the *and*s in a letter than to use *&*s.

WORKSHEET 4 | **Using Hyphens**

EXERCISE A   At the beginning of each sentence, an italicized word has been divided into syllables. On the lines provided, write each word as it should be divided at the end of a line. If a word should not be divided, write the whole word.

EXAMPLES   *u su al ly* **1.** After school, my friends and I _____*usual-*_____ _____*ly*_____ walk straight home.

books   **2.** After we have a snack, we get our _____*books*_____ and study.

pho to graphs   **1.** On every wall in the house were old _____ _____ of our Korean ancestors.

noise   **2.** "Will you please," Mother asked politely, "stop that _____ _____?"

e rase   **3.** If you make a mistake, simply stop and _____ _____ it.

o pin ion   **4.** Everyone in the school has been invited to give an _____ _____ about the new rules.

rec i pe   **5.** Your dinner will turn out fine if you follow each _____ _____ carefully.

EXERCISE B   On the line provided, spell the number before each of the following sentences, using a hyphen if it is needed.

EXAMPLES   *13* **1.** How many dollars are _____*thirteen*_____ quarters?

31 **2.** My uncle has _____*thirty-one*_____ cows on his farm.

22   **1.** My brother turns _____ this weekend.

56   **2.** Only _____ more days until vacation!

73   **3.** Our school band has _____ instruments.

14   **4.** When Eric was _____, he started violin lessons.

42   **5.** This record of Scottish bagpipe music is older than my mom, and she's _____.

LANGUAGE HANDBOOK **14** **PUNCTUATION**

WORKSHEET 5 **Test**

EXERCISE A On the line provided, rewrite each of the following expressions, using the possessive case.

EXAMPLE **1.** the hours of the store *the store's hours* _____

1. the tops of the boxes _____

2. the bone of the dog _____

3. fault of one _____

4. rights of the women _____

5. the parables of Jesus _____

6. a salary of a week _____

7. dictionary that is his _____

8. the coaches of the two teams _____

9. the habit of the deer _____

10. opinion of everyone _____

EXERCISE B On the line provided, write the contraction for the italicized word, words, or number in each of the following sentences.

EXAMPLE _____*Who's*_____ **1.** *Who is* the boss here?

_____ **1.** The twins were born in *1999*.

_____ **2.** Please *do not* stare at me.

_____ **3.** *Where is* the office?

_____ **4.** I know *it is* a smart horse.

_____ **5.** The choir *has not* learned that song.

_____ **6.** *You will* like the Singer story.

_____ **7.** *There is* a rainbow over the house.

_____ **8.** Ira *cannot* go to the bar mitzvah.

_____ **9.** *I am* feeling great today!

_____ **10.** We arrived home at ten *of the clock*.

Continued ☞

EXERCISE C   Add apostrophes and hyphens where they are needed in the following sentences. If a sentence is already correct, write *C* on the line provided.

EXAMPLES   _____ **1.** The Z's are printed in large type.

_____ **2.** Fifty-five people came to the wedding.

_____ **1.** How many @s are in an e-mail address?

_____ **2.** Put one half cup of milk in the rice.

_____ **3.** Your address contains many *8*s.

_____ **4.** How many *you know*s did the speaker use?

_____ **5.** They're not ready for the party.

_____ **6.** We counted thirty nine red cars.

_____ **7.** The shouted *Yea*s meant victory.

_____ **8.** "They wont listen to me!" Jon cried.

_____ **9.** What was the twenty fifth state admitted to the Union?

_____ **10.** Were almost ready to go.

EXERCISE D   Hyphenate the following words where they may be divided at the end of a line. Rewrite the word without a hyphen if it cannot be divided.

EXAMPLES   _____ *cav-ern* _____ **1.** cavern

_____ *young* _____ **2.** young

_____ **1.** today

_____ **2.** intestine

_____ **3.** half

_____ **4.** cousin

_____ **5.** transportation

_____ **6.** north

_____ **7.** fleeting

_____ **8.** zebra

_____ **9.** beginner

_____ **10.** tortoise

LANGUAGE HANDBOOK 15 SPELLING

| WORKSHEET 1 | **Using Word Parts**

EXERCISE   On the line provided, divide each of the following words into parts (prefixes, roots, and suffixes), and write a definition based on the meanings of the parts. Check your definition in a dictionary.

EXAMPLE **1.** disuse _dis|use_   _to stop using_ _____

1. golden _____

2. insupportable _____

3. wishful _____

4. reprint _____

5. happiness _____

6. invisible _____

7. semimonthly _____

8. biped _____

9. prideful _____

10. illogical _____

11. report _____

12. distasteful _____

13. witless _____

14. disobey _____

15. lighten _____

16. vision _____

17. impede _____

18. illegal _____

19. portable _____

20. semidarkness _____

21. restriction _____

22. widen _____

23. pedal _____

24. revert _____

25. earthen _____

LANGUAGE HANDBOOK **15** **SPELLING**

| WORKSHEET 2 | **Using Spelling Rules**

EXERCISE A Fill in the lines provided with the correct letters: *ie, ei, cede, ceed,* or *sede*.

EXAMPLE 1. w _ei_ ght

1. n_____ghbor
2. p_____
3. super_____
4. s_____ze
5. br_____f
6. se_____
7. r_____gn
8. _____ght
9. pr_____stly
10. suc_____

11. rec_____ving
12. bel_____ve
13. w_____rd
14. anc_____nt
15. re_____
16. rel_____f
17. conc_____ted
18. n_____ther
19. fr_____ndly
20. ex_____

EXERCISE B Draw a line through the incorrectly spelled words containing *ie* or *ei* or ending in *cede, ceed,* and *sede* in the following sentences. Then, write the correct spellings on the lines provided. If a sentence is already correct, write *C*.

EXAMPLE _____*reviewed*_____ 1. The new television show was not ~~reveiwed~~ in yesterday's newspaper.

_____ 1. We're excited about the World Sereis starting next week.

_____ 2. "Mexico is not a foriegn country to me because I was born there," Elias said.

_____ 3. The announcer conceded that the contest was not fair.

_____ 4. I trust my conscience to let me know right from wrong.

_____ 5. Surely the invention of the can preceeded the invention of the can opener.

_____ 6. The new doll superceded Baby Beth in my young sister's affections.

_____ 7. Have you ever seen a picture of the Apache cheif Geronimo?

_____ 8. A good friend doesn't try to decieve you.

_____ 9. The machine quickly prints the reciept for the clerk.

_____ 10. Alvin proceded to tell me what should be done about the problem.

LANGUAGE HANDBOOK **15** SPELLING

| WORSHEET 3 | Adding Prefixes and Suffixes

EXERCISE A   On the line provided, spell each of the following words with the given prefix or suffix.

EXAMPLE **1.** trace + able = ___*traceable*___

1. silly + ness = _____
2. pad + ing = _____
3. un + usual = _____
4. argue + ment = _____
5. ready + ly = _____
6. semi + arid = _____
7. courage + ous = _____
8. day + ly = _____
9. mis + understand = _____
10. tie + ing = _____

11. tune + er = _____
12. sub + atomic = _____
13. pray + ing = _____
14. wax + ed = _____
15. post + natal = _____
16. im + modest = _____
17. cry + ed = _____
18. pretty + ness = _____
19. time + ly = _____
20. doze + ing = _____

EXERCISE B   Draw a line through the incorrect spellings of words with prefixes or suffixes in the following sentences. Then, write the correct spellings on the lines provided. If a sentence is already correct, write *C*.

EXAMPLE ___*dried*___ **1.** The mud bricks for the hut were ~~dryed~~ in the sun.

_____   **1.** Would these sculptures rightly be called postmodern?

_____   **2.** The cat was managable in the carrying case.

_____   **3.** "The gar is the strangeest fish I've ever seen!" Philip exclaimed.

_____   **4.** You can always tell businesses that value old-fashioned friendlyness.

_____   **5.** The Chinese exercises of tai chi are surly good to know.

_____   **6.** "Riding in a canoe may be relaxing, but rowwing isn't," Mari protested.

_____   **7.** The milk spilled across the counter and made an aweful mess.

_____   **8.** The suddeness of Ira's departure surprised everyone at the party.

_____   **9.** I like reading Zora Neale Hurston's African American folk tales.

_____   **10.** The sunny day was perfect for hanging the clean beding on the outside line.

LANGUAGE HANDBOOK 15 SPELLING

| WORSHEET 4 | **Forming the Plurals of Nouns** |

EXERCISE A On the line provided, spell the plural form of each of the following nouns.

EXAMPLE 1. fox ____foxes____

1. contralto _____
2. Morales _____
3. hero _____
4. waltz _____
5. salmon _____
6. toe _____
7. 7 _____
8. chief _____
9. track _____
10. ! _____

11. country _____
12. rodeo _____
13. diary _____
14. Chinese _____
15. love _____
16. Grady _____
17. 1990 _____
18. class _____
19. mouse _____
20. donkey _____

EXERCISE B In each of the following sentences, draw a line through the incorrectly spelled plural noun. Then, write the correct spelling on the line provided. If the sentence is already correct, write *C*.

EXAMPLE ____Gomezes____ 1. I wonder how many ~~Gomezs~~ are in the phone book.

_____ 1. The little boy asked the park ranger if wolfs are really fierce.

_____ 2. The new city and county taxs will help fund educational programs.

_____ 3. Some people don't clearly pronounce *s'* at the end of words.

_____ 4. There were many "ahs" when the designer showed her Yoruban dresses.

_____ 5. "A blue jay—no, two blue jaies—are on the wire," Sandy said.

_____ 6. Laura's two uncles were yardmans for the Santa Fe railroad for many years.

_____ 7. The Mercados still make their own tamales.

_____ 8. We have bought three car radioes in the last three years.

_____ 9. Which of the new comedys is your favorite this season?

_____ 10. The guide told us mooses sometimes cross the highway here.

LANGUAGE HANDBOOK **15** SPELLING

| WORSHEET 5 | Forming the Plurals of Nouns

EXERCISE A   On the line provided, spell the plural form of each of the following nouns.

EXAMPLES   **1.** day _____*days*_____

2. *and* _____*and's*_____

1. O'Malley _____
2. berry _____
3. crush _____
4. sheep _____
5. ladder _____
6. woman _____
7. glass _____
8. *well* _____
9. Sioux _____
10. piano _____

11. child _____
12. roof _____
13. stereo _____
14. 1950 _____
15. bush _____
16. *4* _____
17. way _____
18. tomato _____
19. Ryker _____
20. *#* _____

EXERCISE B   In each of the following sentences, draw a line through the incorrectly spelled plural noun. Then, write the correct spelling on the line provided. If the sentence is already correct, write *C*.

EXAMPLE _____*sharks*_____   **1.** Basking ~~sharkes~~ are found in the northern seas.

_____ **1.** Some people are very uncomfortable making apologys.

_____ **2.** Will all of the men rent their tuxs for the formal wedding?

_____ **3.** The architect planned two bayes on the east and west sides of the house.

_____ **4.** Hawaii Volcanoes National Park includes the impressive Mauna Loa.

_____ **5.** Guppys are popular for aquariums because they are brightly colored.

_____ **6.** An athlete with two coachs can quickly become confused.

_____ **7.** The cargoes of some business planes must be extremely heavy.

_____ **8.** The childs had never before seen American Indian wampum beads.

_____ **9.** "You have too many *and*s at the beginning of sentences," Mrs. Lee said.

_____ **10.** The Chineses celebrate the New Year for four days.

LANGUAGE HANDBOOK 15 SPELLING

| WORKSHEET 6 | **Writing Numbers**

EXERCISE A   On the line provided, spell out each of the following numbers.

EXAMPLES   **1.** 88 _eighty-eight_____
           2. 698 _six hundred ninety-eight_____

1. 6 _____

2. 54 _____

3. 17 _____

4. 600 _____

5. 38 _____

6. 89 _____

7. 1,005 _____

8. 12 _____

9. 21 _____

10. 144 _____

EXERCISE B   In each of the following sentences, draw a line through the incorrect form of a number. Then, write the correct form on the line provided. If the sentence is already correct, write *C*.

EXAMPLES   ___3___   **1.** We will be taking 92 people to the concert on ~~three~~ buses.

          second   **2.** That's the ~~2nd~~ time tonight I've heard that dog barking!

_____   **1.** The recipe calls for 2 onions, four cups of dried pasta, and one hundred twenty-eight ounces of chicken broth.

_____   **2.** My sister will be celebrating her 9th wedding anniversary this year.

_____   **3.** 75 people returned the survey to the pollster.

_____   **4.** Of all the people in the class, 15 had seen the movie *The Wizard of Oz* on television, 6 had seen it in a movie theater, and eight had never seen it at all.

_____   **5.** There are 5,280 feet in a mile.

_____   **6.** Is that the 4th or fifth time you've read *The Hobbit*?

_____   **7.** I found 35 articles about the Civil War in the bibliography.

_____   **8.** Thirty-three people called the observatory to report seeing the comet.

_____   **9.** The newspaper reported that 72 senators voted to overturn the president's veto yesterday.

_____   **10.** He is the 10th person who tried the new product and liked it.

WORKSHEET 7 | Test

_____

EXERCISE A   Draw a line through the incorrectly spelled words in the following
sentences. Then, write the correct spellings on the lines provided. There may be more
than one incorrectly spelled word in a sentence. If a sentence is already correct, write *C*.

EXAMPLE _severely, driving_ **1.** Derek's car was ~~severly~~ damaged, and he
won't be ~~driveing~~ very soon.

_____ **1.** Flys actually are quite interesting creatures to observe.

_____ **2.** "Maybe the elfs came in while we were gone and washed the dishs,"
Dad joked.

_____ **3.** Tennis champion Michael Chang probably has inspired many beginers.

_____ **4.** Wanda is the nineth baby sitter that the Pauleys have hired this year.

_____ **5.** The garage is sturdily built, but the neighbors think it looks rickety.

_____ **6.** The sheeps walk across the field, easyly jump the fences, and munch
the plants in the garden.

_____ **7.** Did you find the missing peices of the puzzle?

_____ **8.** Both of Cora's puppies make crying noises when they're hungry.

_____ **9.** Did Julius Lester's work in the civil rights movement preceed his
writing career?

_____ **10.** Lately 5s have been noticable in my life, and I wonder why.

EXERCISE B   The following paragraph contains ten spelling errors. Draw a line
through each error, and write the correct spelling above it.

EXAMPLE [1] The Lashmets took us to ~~thier~~ *their* favorite Japanese restaurant.

  [1] The Japaneses enjoy eating a dish called sushi. [2] You may already know about
sushi, but we didn't; we were beginers in the art of eating sushi. [3] The Lashmets told us
that sushi consists of small rice cakes stuffed with different kinds of fishes, eggs, or
vegetables. [4] They insisted that we order a vareity of sushi. [5] We agreed, and we
proceded to do so. [6] The waitress brought a plentyful amount on a large platter. [7] Our
vegetable sushi was made of cucumbers, squash, and tomatos. [8] We ate a lot, but still had
some left for two "to go" boxs. [9] Some childs in our group didn't like the vinegar in the
rice. [10] Some of us finally succeded in properly using chopsticks to pick up the sushi.

Continued ☞

EXERCISE C The following paragraph contains ten spelling errors. Draw a line through each error, and write the correct spelling above it.

                                  fascinating
        EXAMPLE [1] The Inuit culture is ~~fascinateing~~!

[1] My brother and I recieved a copy of *The Girl Who Dreamed Only Geese and Other Tales of the Far North*. [2] The book contains storys of the Inuit people. [3] Our modern, computerized world has not superceded these tales. [4] We have learned much about the lifes of people in Inuit villages. [5] Some tales have us laughing, while others keep us cring. [6] My favorite story is about the girl who has the power to dream gooses out of the sky. [7] Believe it or not, that's not the wierdest story in the book. [8] My brother likes the tales about heros and the story of the sea gull who wants to be human. [9] The author, Howard Norman, actualy gathered tales from Inuit storytellers. [10] The colorful illustrationes by Leo and Diane Dillon were inspired by Inuit stonecut art.

EXERCISE D Draw a line through the incorrectly spelled words in the following sentences. Then, write the correct spellings on the lines provided. There may be more than one incorrectly spelled word in a sentence. If a sentence is already correct, write *C*.

       EXAMPLE <u>*rallies, extremely*</u> **1.** The youth ~~rallyes~~ are always ~~extremly~~ uplifting experiences.

_____ 1. The minnows looked liked miniature torpedos in the water.

_____ 2. The funniest joke I've heard is about the number of moose needed to change a light bulb.

_____ 3. Chile and Peru are two of the countrys in South America.

_____ 4. The high tide will receed later today.

_____ 5. The clown's jollyness greatly exceded the needs of the occasion.

_____ 6. Writers are sometimes told not to use too many /s in their papers.

_____ 7. The ice storm resulted in many broken branchs on big oak trees.

_____ 8. Isaac, a freind from Ghana, gave me a beautiful peice of cotton cloth.

_____ 9. The Taylors, both famous actors, have appeared in cameos in movies produced locally.

_____ 10. When selectting oranges, feel their wieght to determine the juice content.

LANGUAGE HANDBOOK 16 GLOSSARY OF USAGE

WORKSHEET 1 **Common Usage Problems**

EXERCISE Underline the italicized word or expression in parentheses that is correct according to standard or formal usage.

> EXAMPLE **1.** They did (*a lot*, *alot*) more work on the science project.

1. The window was (*busted*, *broken*) by the hail, not by the baseball.

2. We would (*have*, *of*) fixed tacos for supper if you had come over.

3. Did you see (*where*, *that*) tomorrow is the day we have school pictures taken?

4. My aunt moved here from Naples and is going to (*teach*, *learn*) me how to speak Italian.

5. Tasha had the flu last week and still doesn't feel (*well*, *good*).

6. Did you have to carry the books a long (*ways*, *way*)?

7. We had (*all ready*, *already*) studied the map and knew how to get to the beach.

8. When you come back to the house, please (*bring*, *take*) the flower seeds.

9. We divided the almonds (*between*, *among*) the four of us.

10. My cousin (*choose*, *chose*) to write his report on our Hopi culture and ancestry.

11. (*This here*, *This*) silk from India will make a beautiful sari for my mother.

12. Nathan is (*rather*, *kind of*) excited about taking acting lessons.

13. We (*hadn't*, *had*) scarcely any time to get to the gym before the game started.

14. Our neighbors built that fishpond all by (*theirselves*, *themselves*).

15. The person (*whom*, *which*) I most admire is my grandmother, who lives in Ethiopia.

16. Samuel always (*rises*, *raises*) his hand because he knows the answer to everything.

17. Plant that tree (*anywhere*, *anywheres*) in the yard.

18. We'd rather play a board game (*then*, *than*) go to a movie.

19. There are (*fewer*, *less*) piñatas at the market than there were last week.

20. Will the mild winter (*affect*, *effect*) the insect population this summer?

21. You may want to (*accept*, *except*) the offer before it expires.

22. She wanted (*bad*, *badly*) to have a slumber party on her birthday.

23. We had waited for (*a*, *an*) hour for Gregory to arrive.

24. That fish must (*of*, *have*) been one of the largest caught this year.

25. Kareem (*had ought*, *ought*) to be home by 5:00 P.M. since his soccer practice will be over at 4:30.

LANGUAGE
HANDBOOK **16** GLOSSARY OF USAGE

| WORKSHEET 2 | Common Usage Problems

EXERCISE   Underline the italicized word or expression in parentheses that is correct according to standard or formal usage.

EXAMPLE 1. We don't know (<u>why</u>, *how come*) the mail is late.

1. Last week while we were in Florida, we saw (*a, an*) alligator at the side of the road.

2. Victor plays the guitar well, but plays the piano (*badly, bad*).

3. The kitten was (*nowheres, nowhere*) to be found.

4. Are those the (*kind, kinds*) of colored pencils that we need for art class?

5. Julie (*don't, doesn't*) like to walk in the rain.

6. Before travelers go to Mexico, they (*ought, had ought*) to know the value of the peso.

7. Marian, please (*lie, lay*) the book on the table when you finish reading it.

8. Floyd was glad to (*accept, except*) my help with the model plane.

9. The dog wagged (*it's, its*) tail when I walked into the yard.

10. We had to scrape the old paint (*off, off of*) the boat before we could repaint it.

11. Do you want to (*set, sit*) downstairs or on the balcony?

12. Garnet, this (*isn't, ain't*) the flag of Kenya; Kenya's flag is green, red, and black.

13. (*This, This here*) gate won't close.

14. The (*Trevinos, Trevinos they*) moved here from Minneapolis.

15. An agreement was made (*among, between*) Nicole and Tranh.

16. Be sure to bring (*you're, your*) stamp collection to show the class.

17. I (*use, used*) to read science fiction, but now I read mysteries.

18. Is it (*all right, alright*) to compare the growth rates of plants for our science project?

19. I don't know why (*their, they're*) not going on the camping trip.

20. Rex repaired the trampoline frame by (*hisself, himself*).

21. We enjoyed watching the clown, (*which, who*) was in the center ring.

22. Sandy quickly replied to all (*their, there*) requests for tapes of the music.

23. Did you pick up (*them, those*) socks that were on the floor in your room?

24. Is (*that kind, those kind*) of music your favorite?

25. My little sister still colors (*outside of, outside*) the lines.

WORKSHEET 3 | Test

EXERCISE A   Underline the italicized word or expression in parentheses that is correct according to standard or formal usage.

EXAMPLE **1.** What is (*you're*, *your*) best time in the 100-meter race?

1. The book about Sequoyah's development of the Cherokee alphabet is (*somewhere*, *somewheres*) on that bookshelf.

2. The cactus needs (*less*, *fewer*) water than the geranium.

3. (*Its*, *It's*) fascinating to read about the Olmec, Maya, Aztec, and Inca cultures.

4. The tree (*that*, *who*) was struck by lightning fell across our driveway.

5. Marcos must decide (*among*, *between*) attending the concert and going to the game.

6. The water balloon (*burst*, *busted*) as we were filling it.

7. Alinda likes all kinds of tropical fruit (*accept*, *except*) papayas.

8. Do you know (*how come*, *why*) our test was canceled?

9. During Kwanzaa, people joyously celebrate (*they're*, *their*) African heritage.

10. Jovita Gonzalez (*she wrote*, *wrote*) the book *Among My People* about her childhood.

EXERCISE B   Most of the following sentences contain errors in usage. If a sentence contains an error, draw a line through the error and write the correction on the line provided. If a sentence is already correct, write *C*.

EXAMPLE   ___could have___   **1.** If you'd been on time, we ~~could of~~ seen the whole movie.

_____ **1.** My parents they hope to send me to a college.

_____ **2.** A exciting thing has happened! Our team won the quiz bowl.

_____ **3.** Alligators and crocodiles are of the same family but ain't identical.

_____ **4.** Often, the effect of El Niño on the weather is increased rainfall.

_____ **5.** We love to picnic between the many trees in the state park.

_____ **6.** We had to rise the shelf to keep the baby from getting into things.

_____ **7.** Its true that Lake Huron is named for the Indian people who live nearby.

_____ **8.** Boccie, an Italian game, is sort of like lawn bowling.

_____ **9.** Don't everyone know that the mesosphere is above the stratosphere?

_____ **10.** I typed bad until I took typing lessons.

Continued ☞

EXERCISE C   Underline the italicized word or expression in parentheses that is correct according to standard or formal usage.

EXAMPLE **1.** First we drew, and (*than*, *then*) we painted the pictures.

1. When you are (*already*, *all ready*), we will leave for the museum.

2. Whenever I (*lie*, *lay*) down in a hammock, I tip over and fall out.

3. These (*type*, *types*) of brackets are best for holding up shelves.

4. Francois, please (*take*, *bring*) those tapes home when you go.

5. Our dog insists on sleeping on the ground (*outside of*, *outside*) her doghouse.

6. The (*affect*, *effect*) of the space program has been increased interest in the universe.

7. Be careful not to (*sit*, *set*) too close to the campfire.

8. It takes me a long time to (*chose*, *choose*) the correct answer in a workbook.

9. Let's sing some of (*them*, *those*) songs we learned in music class.

10. It's difficult to stay friends with someone who has a (*bad*, *bad*ly) attitude.

EXERCISE D   Most of the following sentences contain errors in usage. If a sentence contains an error, draw a line through the error and write the correction on the line provided. If a sentence is already correct, write *C*.

EXAMPLE _____*book fair?*_____ **1.** Where is the ~~book fair at~~?

_____ 1. You don't have to go all the ways to Japan to study Zen Buddhism.

_____ 2. That there broccoli is ready to put in the soup.

_____ 3. My grandmother learned me how to play cat's cradle with string.

_____ 4. I draw alot of designs for buildings; maybe I should be an architect.

_____ 5. It wasn't hardly worth the effort to climb the hill in the fog.

_____ 6. Dan said your making spiced empanadas for the Cinco de Mayo fiesta.

_____ 7. We should of figured the square feet of wall space before buying paint.

_____ 8. Kim and Lee said their kites and balls of string were somewhere in the closet.

_____ 9. I heard where the science club is needing help with the exhibition.

_____ 10. Just two players will need less marbles for a game of Chinese checkers.